What they're saying about *Vegan U*

Vegan Unplugged provides a unique and important (recipes and strategies for surviving an emergency o there's no going hungry with the Five-Day Meal Box not only help you avert personal health disasters, it will give you all the tools you need to handle any situation that comes your way.

> —Neal Barnard, M.D., President, Physicians Committee for Responsible Medicine

Whether it's a hurricane, earthquake, or just a simple power outage, *Vegan Unplugged* can save the day—it's a survival guide with gourmet sensibilities.

> —Erik Marcus, publisher of Vegan.com and author of *The Ultimate Vegan Guide*

Prepare to meet the new, gourmet style of Pantry Cuisine. *Vegan Unplugged* dishes up flavor and variety with dozens of delicious recipes that can be prepared in minutes, even when the refrigerator is bare. A must-have for any day when your resources are limited or your motivation to cook is waning.

> —Alisa Fleming, author of *Go Dairy Free* and publisher of GoDairyFree.org

From weather-related power disruptions to any need to quickly cobble up a tasty meal, Jon Robertson has a plan that covers these and many other situations when being prepared is the key. By enlisting his wife, well known chef and cookbook author Robin Robertson, the author ensures that regardless of circumstances, delicious dining can still be an option. With Jon's scope of vision and attention to details, his guide calls you to adventure instead of being stuck in a hapless situation.

> —Chef Ken Bergeron, author of *The Professional Vegetarian Chef*

Vegan Unplugged: A Pantry Cuisine and Survival Guide is an insurance policy every family should purchase. It can turn a disaster into an adventure.

—Howard F. Lyman, author of *Mad Cowboy*

Fresh is always best, but in this uncertain world, it's good to know there's a resource to turn to when power outages hit or natural disasters strike. Even when lack of access to a plugged-in kitchen is voluntary (such as while traveling and camping), *Vegan Unplugged* is your go-to source. Jon and Robin Robertson offer a wealth of tips and recipes that make staying with your plant-based diet a breeze – even under the most challenging conditions.

—Nava Atlas, author of *Vegan Express*

In the years to come, it's going to be increasingly important to be able to prepare healthy meals when the power is out and when fresh food is unavailable. *Vegan Unplugged* is a marvelous resource to help you prepare healthy and inexpensive meals using nonperishable ingredients. Highly recommended for those prudent enough to recognize we could be in for a bumpy ride.

— John Robbins, author of *The New Good Life, The Food Revolution,* and *Diet For a New America*

Vegan Unplugged

A Pantry Cuisine Cookbook and Survival Guide

Jon Robertson

with recipes by Robin Robertson

VEGAN HERITAGE PRESS
Woodstock • Virginia

Vegan Unplugged is a comprehensive revision of *Apocalypse Chow: How to Eat Well When the Power Goes Out* by Jon Robertson with Robin Robertson (Simon Spotlight Entertainment, an imprint of Simon & Schuster, ISBN: 978-1-4169-0824-1, © 2005 by Jon Robertson).

First Edition, September 2010

ISBN 13: 978-0-9800131-2-2
ISBN 10: 0-9800131-2-7

Vegan Heritage Press books are available at quantity discounts. For information, please visit our website at www.veganheritagepress.com or write the publisher at Vegan Heritage Press, P.O. Box 628, Woodstock, VA 22664-0628.

Publisher's Note: The information in this book is true and complete to the best of our knowledge. Website addresses and contact information were correct at the time of publication. The publisher is not responsible for specific health or allergy needs that may require medical supervision, nor adverse reactions to recipes contained in this book. The authors and publisher disclaim all liability in connection with the use of the book.

Printed in the United States of America

Contents

Acknowledgements

A number of individuals and organizations played a role in the creation of this book. Special appreciation goes to Robin Robertson, for her good humor, culinary guidance, and creative pantry recipes. Grateful appreciation goes to Jenna Patton and Samantha Ragan for their perceptive insights and fine editing skills. Thanks also to Anna West and Russell Patton for their timely ideas. Also to be acknowledged are the American Red Cross; the Federal Emergency Management Agency (FEMA); the National Weather Service (NWS); the U.S. Department of Homeland Security; the U.S. Department of Agriculture (USDA); the U.S. Department of Health and Human Services (HHS); the Humane Society of the United States; and the International Guild of Professional Butlers.

Introduction

We all know that fresh food is the best food. Unfortunately, there are occasions when fresh either isn't available or there's no time to prepare it. *Vegan Unplugged* gives you solutions for those times. It brings to your table the amazingly simple Pantry Cuisine—delicious recipes that are quick and easy to make from healthy ingredients found in your pantry.

This book is a concise, helpful guide for any time when cooking becomes a challenge. It can be used when you're on the road, visiting nonvegan relatives, or taking that long-awaited camping trip. It can help you when you're ill, when you just don't feel like cooking, or whenever the power is out.

Vegan Unplugged will save the day with Robin Robertson's eighty clever Pantry Cuisine recipes that can be made in just a few minutes. Known for her fine cookbooks using fresh ingredients, Robin has created great flavors and textures in recipes that can be made strictly from nonperishable pantry ingredients.

These recipes leave typical "survival food" in the dust by providing full-flavored soups, entrees, salads, and snacks. Who wouldn't prefer Artichoke, Shiitake and White Bean Soup (page 131), Rice Noodles with Spicy Peanut Sauce (page 97), or some Garlicky Chickpeas with Potatoes and Tomatoes (page 66) to a tasting menu of peanut butter crackers, potato chips, and energy bars? Each recipe requires a minimum of preparation, cooking time, and clean-up in order to keep things simple and, in emergency situations, help you conserve precious fuel and water for cooking and drinking.

Vegan Unplugged shows you how to stock a fine Pantry Stash. It also shows you how to assemble the amazing Five-Day Meal Box—your go-to food box for road trips, hotel stays, and camping trips. But *Vegan Unplugged* is more than just a fabulous Pantry Cuisine cookbook. It's also a preparedness guide for any emergency situation in which the power is out or any time you don't have fresh ingredients.

Whenever you find yourself without refrigeration and having to rely on pantry ingredients, *Vegan Unplugged* will help you to "make the most of it" when you have to "make the best of it."

Vegan Unplugged is a comprehensive revision of *Apocalypse Chow: How to Eat Well When the Power Goes Out* (Simon Spotlight, 2005). The recipes are fully vegan (with twelve new ones). This book offers updated information, helpful sidebars, and a concise emergency preparedness guide. *Vegan Unplugged* also includes a new section on dealing with stress, a resources list, and how to care for your animal companions during an emergency.

When You're Unplugged

*V*egan Unplugged is the first vegan Pantry Cuisine cookbook and emergency preparedness guide. It is intended to be the go-to resource for vegans (and non-vegans, too) to make delicious, nutritious meals no matter what situation prevents you from eating fresh food. Whether it's a long hotel stay, camping, boating, being too busy to cook, away at school, or even if you're cooking challenged, this book can come to the rescue.

Vegan Unplugged is also your best resource for any emergency situation in which you've lost power due to a storm, hurricane, or other act of nature. If you have ever lived without electrical power for a couple of days or more, you know the mealtime privation that comes with it. In a time of increasingly unpredictable

weather and evermore powerful natural events, being prepared for emergencies is everyone's business. This may be especially true for vegans, for whom traveling or even a weekend visit with nonvegan relatives can constitute a mealtime emergency.

Let's begin with what happened to us after Hurricane Isabel back in 2003 and how this book came to be.

Lessons from Isabel

After Hurricane Isabel hit Virginia Beach, we endured over a week without electricity—days in which we not only ate nutritious food, but ate excellent gourmet-style meals in the bargain. Here's what happened:

The day before Isabel hit, the hurricane was already hammering North Carolina's Outer Banks. The bellies of the leaves showed white against the slate gray sky as we screwed plywood over our windows, a job that required most of a day and a lot of cursing. The smell of ozone spiced the air, and the oceanfront was cast in a foreboding yellow glow.

My wife, Robin, and I had done all the customary preparation that people who live on the coast generally follow: a good supply of wine, red and white, including a serviceable Pinot Noir for storm refugees who might enjoy it. People do this all along the coast because so many storms turn into near misses or amount to little more than hard wind and a good soaking.

We trekked out to the supermarket for extra water, food, and flashlight batteries—just in case this was the Big One. The canned meats section was crowded, but we were bound for greener pastures. We loaded up on the standard issue water jugs and paper products, of course, but Robin started tossing food items into the cart that seemed more appropriate for a dinner party than a hurricane.

"Remember Hurricane Bonnie?" she called over her shoulder. During that storm, we were caught offguard and had subsisted for four days on peanut butter crackers and little else. "Never again," had become our battle cry.

In the checkout line, our cart contrasted sharply with those around us. Furtively judging the other people's preparedness (everyone peeks), we noticed a preponderance of prepared canned foods: SpaghettiOs, Spam, and canned stew, along with white bread, chips, cheeze doodles, and plenty of beer. Frowns turned our way as suspicious eyes inspected our marinated artichoke hearts, dried shiitakes, capellini, and couscous. Robin, a vegan cookbook author and former chef, had a plan: We were used to eating fabulous meals morning, noon, and night with the electricity on, and we were determined to do so even without electricity.

Isabel turned out to have been only a Category 2 storm, but the neighborhood was trashed and some houses had been cleaved in two by trees. Fortunately for us, the actual damage to our property was minor—some broken shingles, one humongous pine tree crushed twenty feet of fence and some outside coach lights. We were relieved that the hurricane was over, but the ordeal of living without electrical power had only just begun.

Long about lunchtime, our strategy paid off. Robin fired up a portable butane stove and made a comforting vegetable soup with the remains of our fresh produce. In so doing, we observed one of the first principles of emergency preparedness: When the power goes out, eat up the fresh produce first followed by the frozen.

Later that day, we worked together to prepare our evening meal. Before long I was up to my elbows in minced garlic and beans, and mentally occupied with something besides the storm for the first time in two days.

The city's water was still running, so we washed the dishes and retired to the living room, oil lamp and radio in hand, where, try as I might, lack of light made it impossible to read. Not even my newly issued Hubble-power bifocals would allow it. There was no TV. No books. Just the chatter of the spastic news announcer as Isabel tore up the coast north of us.

Then began something we knew all too well: endless days of crushing boredom in the relentless Virginia heat and humidity. Add to that the angry screams of ear-splitting generators and chain saws. Where to run? Our only escape from the noise was inside our hot, cave-like house, so sitting out on the patio and struggling to get through a book became a test of nerves. Word was that power wouldn't be restored for two weeks. We stared into the abyss of a dark, hot house, having nothing to do, with no hot water, air conditioning, computers, videos, or food processor.

Through all of that commotion, grinding boredom, and noise, however, we were determined to eat well, and we did. Nightly, we dined at sunset on impossibly good vegan meals made in fifteen minutes or less. Why so quick? Because we had to conserve our butane fuel. We used meal preparation to "cook through the boredom," and incorporated hand-washing dishes as part of our "busy-work" each day.

Vegans Unplugged

We came up with this strategy as a result of being unplugged involuntarily, but the same strategy can be applied to a host of domestic situations in which you may find yourself without access to fresh, refrigerated, or frozen food. This book shows you how to make great meals with pantry ingredients, as well as how to prepare for a variety of situations. Here are some examples gleaned from the vicissitudes of daily life.

Road Trips

How many times have you found yourself on the interstate, freeway, or country road and realized how hungry you were, only to further realize that the nearest vegan restaurant may as well be a thousand miles away? A show of hands would reveal that vegans of every stripe have been there and done that.

Whenever you travel, it's a good idea to scout on the Internet in advance for vegan-friendly restaurants along your travel route. We always do online research before we leave home, so we know what to expect. Most cities and larger towns have vegan restaurants or places that offer a few vegan-friendly menu items. Chinese, Thai, Indian, or Vietnamese restaurants offering vegan options are plentiful nowadays, so travel is generally much easier than it used to be.

There are times, however, when you're bound for territories with no vegan dining whatsoever. In these situations, you may be limited to the old stand-by: a Taco Bell bean burrito, fresco style (salsa, no cheese). Once, out of desperation, we wandered into a Cracker Barrel and were nearly seduced into ordering the "vegetable plate"— only to discover that most of the vegetable sides were laced with ham or bacon. We had to make do with a tossed salad and applesauce.

You can always ensure a happy and healthy road trip by keeping a cooler in the backseat of the car filled with prepared foods such as sandwiches, hummus, cut vegetables, fruit, energy bars, and drinks. For extended trips where vegan options are dismal, take with you the Five-Day Meal Box described in Chapter 2. You'll eat well whether you're in a campground or hotel.

Hotels

If you can book a room with a kitchenette, you'll be able to cook vegan meals just like at home. If you can, plan your meals in advance and bring the Five-Day Meal Box with you. Armed with your copy of *Vegan Unplugged*, you'll be able to cook up some comfort foods in your home-away-from-home. Note: if bringing your own ingredients is impractical, consider shopping at a local market for your provisions once you arrive at your destination. If you can't get a room with a kitchenette, you will still be able to cook for yourself, though you'd want to bring with you an electric single-burner stove rather than the butane open-flame type.

Visiting Relatives

Are you going home to visit the folks? Anticipating dinner with your significant other's parents? Have you been invited to a family reunion camping weekend? Scenarios like these can strike fear in the hearts of intrepid vegans, but Pantry Cuisine can come to the rescue.

Even when our omnivore friends and relatives are trying to be gracious, they sometimes can't wrap their heads around the concept of no animal products. The vegetables might be swimming in butter; the bean soup might have been made with chicken broth; the cake will almost certainly contain eggs.

Depending on your relationship with your hosts and the duration of your visit, you might consider these options:

- Eat before you go
- Bring your own prepared foods
- Provide your hosts with a list of ingredients they can swap out if they want to be really accommodating (Earth Balance, soy milk, vegetable broth, etc.)
- Send your hosts a simple recipe or two that they can prepare
- Offer to do your own cooking while visiting

The solution that works best for us is to bring our own ingredients (or shop when we arrive) and cook for ourselves. We usually make enough food to share with our hosts to show them how good vegan food can be.

Too Busy to Cook?

Many people work constantly, meaning long days and long weeks. This seems to be true whether they're working in business, Internet, or creative work. These quick Pantry Cuisine recipes are of great help to anyone in this situation. I know a graduate student who was working feverishly on her doctoral dissertation in the winter of 2010. The deadlines had her working long days with little time for cooking. To get through it, she prepared many of these recipes, and they saved her a lot of time.

Sick at Home

Maybe you don't mind cooking, but suppose you're home sick from work or school. The fridge is empty, and you just don't feel like cooking, much less shopping. Here's another reason to have a Pantry Stash in the house (see Chapter 3). The recipes in this book are easy, and they can all be made in 15 minutes or less. With a minimum of effort, you can be enjoying a hot bowl of homemade soup that can help you get your strength back.

Are You Cooking-Challenged?

Some people don't like cooking or have never learned how. But you've still gotta eat. If your refrigerator is bare and your finger is sprained from dialing for take-out, the easy recipes in this book may be just what you need. Open a few cans, heat, and eat. With a little practice, you might even get to like cooking.

What would be more confidence building to the culinary-challenged than touching off a pair of long white tapers and serving Instant Vichyssoise (page 125), Wild Mushroom Rice Pilaf (page 92), and No-Fuss Chocolate Fondue (page 152), all made in minutes with little mess and without any appreciable knowledge of cooking?

A note to singles and couples cooking out of your Pantry Stash: As most of the recipes in this book serve four modest portions, two people with voracious appetites can polish off many of the recipes without help, but others may find it helpful to cut recipes in half.

Back to School

While students are rarely without electricity, the sad irony is that they choose not to use it for doing their own cooking. Eating habit reports from college campuses aren't good. Students have been known to wash down Hot Pockets with soda or blur-spoon Cap'n Crunch. Vegan students have it particularly tough where fast-food and convenience foods are concerned.

Let Pantry Cuisine come to the rescue by providing quick and cheap nutrition in a delicious meal with easy clean-up. Make black bean chili, corn chowder, blueberry cobbler, and dozens of other gourmet-quality recipes in fifteen minutes. Pantry Cuisine is especially easy if you have a microwave in your room (see Microwave Modifications on page 40). This also goes for students who rent a room, whose sustenance relies on a single shelf in the refrigerator downstairs, or those who have an apartment in town. If you have a stove, use a pan instead of the microwave. Whether you're a freshman or grad student, these recipes can provide proper nutrition when you're on the go.

Boating

Boaters have to be choosy about their onboard stowage. That's where the techniques in this book are invaluable. The store-bought nonperishables in your Five-Day Meal Box larder (see Chapter 2) won't take up much space. Even if you're all thumbs in the kitchen, you can dazzle your shipmates with great meals in less than 15 minutes.

Camping

Using the recipes in this book can inspire even the most rugged individuals to ratchet up the quality of their meals while they're away from civilization. Many years ago, Robin and I and four friends decided to try camping. We were townies who didn't know the difference between a tent peg and a camp stove, but we bought some cheapo equipment and went camping under the stars at Hickory Run State Park in northeastern Pennsylvania.

Along with our tent and some pans, it seemed perfectly natural to bring a one-gallon cooler of dry Bombay martinis—1 tablespoon vermouth to 1 gallon gin. On checking into the park, the ranger peeked through the windows of our car and muttered, "You folks ever go camping before?"

Too proud to admit that we were tinhorns, we fumbled with struts, lines, and pegs, and had to start over a couple of times. Sure, we were amateur campers, but we were expert eaters. On our picnic table, we placed two three-taper silver candelabras atop a starched white tablecloth. For dinner that first night, we made linguine with a fresh tomato and basil sauce, a salad of torn greens and toasted pine nuts with a garlicky vinaigrette. For dessert, we made a cherry clafouti cooked in a skillet over a wood fire. Surrounded by experienced campers who were roasting hot dogs and marshmallows on sticks, grilling burgers, or heating cans of soup, we only began to feel self-conscious the next day after one of us visited a neighboring camp site, inquiring of the jack-booted wilderness types if they could spare a garlic press.

The above field research shows how, with clever recipes and a little planning, you can turn any rustic clearing into a Michelin Four Star-rated chef's table.

SPECIAL ADVICE FOR NON-VEGANS

Non-vegans take note: When the power is out, the foods that are most dangerous to you and your family will be the meats, eggs, and dairy products slowly warming in your fridge and freezer. For this reason, you should take a special interest in this book, from the Pantry Cuisine menus and recipes to the Emergency Preparedness Guide in Chapter 12. Even with the electricity on, you can't beat a diet of plant-based food for the health and welfare of your family, the animals, and the planet.

Remodeling

It was barely five months after Hurricane Isabel, in the winter of 2004, when Robin and I were able to put her Pantry Cuisine to the test. We were without power once again for several days, only this time due to a disaster of another type: We were adding a second floor to a portion of our house, installing central heat and air, and upgrading the electrical service. The project took months. The day-to-day construction was nerve-wracking enough, as we'd packed ourselves into a couple of small crowded rooms for the duration. We'd been at it two months already when the day came to switch over the power. It was supposed to take three hours but took three days instead.

Throughout the ordeal, we were determined to rely on our resourcefulness, using what we'd invented during Isabel to come through the three days well-fed and happy—at least well-fed. We whipped out some primitive writing tools (a tablet and pen), and, with the help of our oil lamp, our Pantry Stash, and Robin's single-burner butane stove, we pressed on with various editorial assignments.

How Pantry Cuisine Can Help

Whatever the circumstances that lead you to Pantry Cuisine, *Vegan Unplugged* can be your best friend. In the next few chapters, you will discover how to stock your Pantry Stash with practical menus for making the eighty Pantry Cuisine recipes in the book. You will also find a grocery list for putting together a special Five-Day Meal Box that will feed four people for five days, and that all fits into a lidded plastic box.

Various cooking methods are described for making these amazingly tasty meals, though all can be adapted for preparation with a conventional stove or microwave. These chapters will also explain how to use what you have on-hand

and how to determine when fresh or thawing food is unsafe. Also discussed are what I call "SRCs" (supermarket ready-to-cooks, see Chapter 3), which are freeze-dried, dehydrated foods, and convenience products.

Finally, *Vegan Unplugged* features a concise Emergency Preparedness Guide that shows you how to prepare for any lengthy power outage. Chapters 12 and 13 provide a concise Disaster Supply List and Family Plan, as well as a plan for taking good care of the companion animals in your life. With *Vegan Unplugged,* you will be prepared for any extended stretch without power. You'll make great, quick meals and be glad you used the emergency preparedness guide to be ready for any loss of electrical power, whether by choice or necessity.

Pantry Cuisine enables anyone to get dinner on the table without a food processor or microwave. Use the handy sidebars, tips, and Resources directory to keep your household well fed, amused, and healthy. The book also offers suggestions on how to keep your sanity through the boring wait until power is restored.

The next chapter gets you started on your Five-Day Meal Box, which has produced *Aha!* moments for vegans and nonvegans alike. It's a handy resource that takes the guesswork out of meal planning any time you have to be away from fresh food for an extended period of time.

2

The Five-Day Meal Box

The Five-Day Meal Box takes the guesswork out of emergency preparedness by giving you all you need for cooking great meals without electricity. It can also be used for road trips, hotel stays, or camping trips.

The innovation is that these items allow two to four people (depending on your appetites) to eat breakfast, lunch, and dinner for five days. The menus and shopping list are ready to use, and the items fit into a 50-quart Rubbermaid lidded container with room to spare. This box works great because it takes up so little space. Since the ingredients are nonperishable, it can be hidden in the bottom of a linen closet, in the basement, in the galley of a boat, a dorm room, or in any other out-of-the-way corner.

And what's the cost of these goodies? About $70. That's not bad to get up to four people through fifteen meals without electricity. Please note that about $15 of the cost is for the breakfast items alone. Without those, you can fit your provisions into a smaller box for about $55. With breakfast included, these meals cost about $1.18 per meal per person, so it's an economical way to eat.

The Five-Day Meal Box

As you look over the menu, be aware that our recipe list reflects our taste. To personalize your list, simply flip through the book and choose the recipes you like, then revise the grocery list. You can prepare additional boxes, either for more people or more days by doubling the grocery list. Remember that while the menu suggests recipes for well-balanced, one-dish meals for breakfast, lunch, and dinner, it does not include additional side dishes, desserts, or beverages. Also keep in mind that without refrigeration, you can't save leftovers. If you are a couple or a single person, consider cutting the recipes in half or adapting the recipes for fewer portions.

The Five-Day Menu

Day 1

Breakfast: Oatmeal with raisins
Lunch: Comforting Corn Chowder (page 130) and Beat-the-Blahs Black
  Bean Patties (page 72)
Dinner: Kitchen-Sink Capellini (page 82)

Day 2

Breakfast: Cream of Wheat with agave and slivered almonds
Lunch: White Beans and Greens Soup (page 121)
Dinner: Almost-Instant Black Bean Chili (page 67)

Day 3

Breakfast: Oatmeal with cinnamon
Lunch: Niçoise Salad (page 113)
Dinner: Curry in a Hurry (page 73)

Day 4

Breakfast: Cream of Wheat with raisins and agave
Lunch: Composed Marinated Vegetable Salad (page 108) and Texas Twister
  Caviar (page 139)
Dinner: Pasta with White Beans and Olivada (page 87)

Day 5

Breakfast: Oatmeal with agave, raisins, and cinnamon
Lunch: Five-Minute Couscous Salad (page 103)
Dinner: Layered Tortilla Skillet (page 93)

Grocery List for the Five-Day Menu

1 (15.5-ounce) can kidney beans
3 (15.5-ounce) cans black beans
2 (15.5-ounce) cans pinto beans
2 (15.5-ounce) cans chickpeas
2 (15.5-ounce) cans white beans
1 (15.5-ounce) can black-eyed peas
5 (14.5-ounce) cans diced tomatoes
3 (15-ounce) cans corn kernels or 2
 cups dehydrated
5 (15-ounce) cans white potatoes or
 3 cups dehydrated potatoes
1 (8-ounce) can spinach or 1/2 cup
 dehydrated
2 (15-ounce) cans plus 1 (8-ounce)
 can green beans or 1 1/2 cups
 dehydrated
2 (16-ounce) jars three-bean salad
2 (4-ounce) cans diced green chiles
1 (8-ounce) jar kalamata olives
2 (4-ounce) cans sliced black olives
2 (6-ounce) jars marinated artichoke
 hearts
2 (16-ounce) jars salsa
1 (4-ounce) jar roasted red bell peppers
1 package flour tortillas

4 ramen noodle bricks
1 pound capellini pasta
1 box couscous
1 (8-ounce) carton non-dairy milk
1 package vegetable bullion
 cubes or powdered soup base
1 small bottle lemon juice
1 small bottle vinegar
1 small bottle olive oil
1 box instant oatmeal
1 box instant Cream of Wheat
1 small container agave nectar
1 box raisins
1 jar instant coffee
tea bags

*Measured into small sealed
 plastic bags:*
1/2 cup tiny pasta for soup
3/4 cup dried breadcrumbs
1/2 cup slivered almonds
1/2 cup sun-dried tomatoes
1 tablespoon cornstarch
Spices for recipes (see note on
 the next page)

NOTE: You probably already have spices in the house. Consider portioning small amounts of the specified spices in small plastic bags or a days-of-the-week pill container. They should tuck easily in the nooks and crannies around the other ingredients and be ready for any occasion. For these recipes you'll need: basil, cayenne, celery salt, chili powder, chives, cinnamon, curry powder, garlic powder, marjoram, dry mustard, savory, dehydrated onion, oregano, parsley, red pepper flakes, salt, and pepper. You will also need one bulb of fresh garlic on hand (do not store long term).

Making Breakfast

In the Five-Day Meal Box, we include a basic breakfast of instant hot cereals, since they store easily, don't take up too much space, and require no cooking (just hot water). When using food from your pantry (as opposed to the meal box), your breakfast options can increase to include other types of cereals, pancake mix, peanut butter, juice, and energy bars. Our emergency breakfast usually consists of oatmeal, toast with peanut butter (made with bread we had on hand), and coffee. For the cereal, we use soy milk from small aseptic containers, but you can mix your own soy or rice milk from powder instead. To make toast, we just hold a piece of bread over the butane flame with long metal kitchen tongs.

> ### NO COFFEE MAKER?
>
> A small jar of instant coffee is included in the Five-Day Meal Box. However, if only fresh coffee will do, you have a few options. A French press does a great job when you're without electricity, but you could instead go the "cowboy way" by boiling water with ground coffee in a saucepan then straining it through a fine mesh strainer or paper coffee filter.

An "Extras" Box

The Five-Day Meal Box menus provide complete meals, but you may also want to set aside an "extras" box to improve your basic experience. In this box, you will include snacks, desserts, and beverages, and a few other items to round out the meals. Following is a list of suggested extras; however, you can customize it according to your preferences:

Recipe "extras":
crackers and other bread items (for soups, salads, etc.)
gardiniara salad and caponata (for the pasta dishes)
tortilla chips (for the chili)

Other breakfast items:
granola, pancake mix, breakfast bars, peanut butter, etc.

Snacks and desserts:
canned fruit, cookies, nuts, energy bars, trail mix, and other treats

"Just in case" items:
If you have room in the box, toss in a jar of pasta sauce and a box of pasta. Maybe stash a few extra bricks of ramen noodles, and a couple of "heat and eat" Supermarket Ready-to-Cooks of your choosing (see SRCs on page 31).

Beverages of choice

NOTE: Water is not included in this list, but make sure you stock up on more water than you think you will need in case your water gets turned off or is undrinkable during an emergency. See page 23 for suggestions.

If You're Leaving Home

When you're taking your Five-Day Meal Box on the road, unless your destination has a working kitchen, you will appreciate having some basic kitchen items to prepare the meals while you're away. Before you leave, you will want to grab a skillet, saucepan, can opener, your portable butane stove, dishwashing soap, and a plastic basin. Naturally, if you'll be cooking at home, these items will already be in place in your kitchen. In the event of a mandatory evacuation, having everything in one place and ready to go will save you time at the last minute.

In addition to being ideal for emergency situations, the Five-Day Meal Box is also great for college students, boaters, and campers. As with any pantry larder, the nonperishable canned and boxed foods should be rotated after one year.

3

The Pantry Stash

With your Five-Day Meal Box safely stored and ready to grab at a moment's notice, you'll still want to outfit your pantry for general use in making Pantry Cuisine at home. This chapter gives you the Pantry Stash, a practical list of additional vegan nonperishables to stock up on, along with some helpful strategies that Robin and I learned during our hurricane years. (We moved to the mountains in 2007, but now have to deal with ice and snowstorms instead.) The chapter will enable you to put food on the table in minutes, no matter why you're reaching for pantry meals, and also be prepared for an extended loss of electricity. It's all about gathering a specific range of shelf-stable ingredients, those that can be stored at room temperature without spoiling.

Personalizing Your Pantry

You don't have to purchase everything in the Pantry Stash list or even great quantities of any particular item. If it's a power failure that you're preparing for, consider the typical causes in your location. This will help determine how much food to buy. If you live in Chicago, odds are you'll never experience a hurricane, but an icy wind storm or blizzard is surely headed your way, if not this year, then the next.

If you're only squirreling away enough provender to get through a thunderstorm, you'll need a smaller pantry stash than someone who is hedging his bet against a category 5 hurricane. Another pantry factor is the number of people in your household. If it's just one or two of you, then buy ingredients in smaller amounts, and leave the buying-club skid of #10 cans for the Brady bunch down the street.

You will want to tailor the list to your likes and dislikes (and those of your family), your needs, and the area in which you live. Choose menus and recipes that you like and buy ingredients only for those recipes. The decisions to be made are mostly logical: If you don't buy ingredients you don't like,then buy double what you do like so you have enough ingredients to make everything at least twice. In addition to planning for specific recipes in Chapters 6-11, your list should also include additional items you will use, such as juices, canned and dried fruits, cereals, and snack foods, as well as specialty items for infants, children, or the elderly.

The following list is a roster of foods and other items you should stock up on before you need them. Since everyone's situation is different, you will want to use the list as a guideline and customize it to suit your needs by listing specific ingredients and quantities your family will eat within each of the categories. After the general list are suggestions for nonperishable international groceries that you may also want to include.

Naturally, your pantry will already include items you use regularly (when you're plugged in) such as longer cooking grains, dried beans, etc.

The list is meant to augment your regular pantry items. Think of it as a checklist of common essential items for short-term preparedness. Use it as a guide to make a list of ingredients for specific meals that your family will enjoy. On your own shopping list, note the quantities of each item you will need to feed the number of people in your family for as long as a week. Included in this list should be the ingredients necessary to make particular Pantry Cuisine recipes that you want to make. Buy only as much as your storage space and budget will allow. For convenience, you can make a copy of this list to customize for your own needs or type up your own list on your computer using this list as a guide.

> ### "WATER, WATER EVERYWHERE..."
>
> Plan on 1 gallon of water per person per day for drinking, cooking, and brushing teeth. Include enough water for companion animals, too. If you rely on tap water, make it bacterially safe by boiling it for 2 minutes before using. You could then run it through a water pitcher equipped with a filter (such as the Brita brand) to remove other pollutants.

Checklist for a Pantry Stash

Beverages:
water, bottled (1 gallon per person per day)
fruit and vegetable juices
non-dairy milk (aseptic boxes and powdered)
cocoa powder
instant coffee
tea bags
wine and beer (optional)

Breakfast Foods:
ready-to-eat cereals
instant or quick-cooking hot cereals: oatmeal, Cream of Wheat, etc.
pancake mix

Comfort Foods/Snacks:
fruits: canned and dried (a variety)
nuts and seeds (a variety)
peanut butter
vegan cookies
energy bars
vegan chocolate bars and chips
trail mix
hard candy, lollipops

Grains, Pasta, Noodles:
bulgur
couscous
pasta (quick-cooking): angel hair, cappelini, orzo

noodles: ramen, rice, lasagna
polenta (prepared shelf-stable box or tube or instant mix)
instant grits
kasha
quick-cooking rice

Prepared Foods (canned, boxed, etc.):

canned beans (variety)
pickled vegetables, canned and jarred
refried beans
prepared salads: three-bean salad, caponata, etc.
soups (cans, boxes, packets, or instant cups)
tofu, silken (in aseptic packages)
canned tomato products (puree, sauce, diced, whole, paste)
texturized soy protein
canned vegetables (variety)
dehydrated vegetables (variety)

Breads, Crackers, Flour:

bread products: breadsticks, assorted crackers, etc.
canned brown bread
taco shells
tortillas
all-purpose flour
vital wheat gluten
cornstarch
baking powder

Cooking sauces and other liquids:

marinara sauce

barbecue sauce
oils: canola oil, olive oil, sesame oil
coconut milk
cooking wines: sherry, mirin, etc.
lemon juice and lime juice
maple syrup and/or agave nectar
salsa
Tabasco sauce
tamari or other soy sauce
teriyaki sauce
vinegars: balsamic, apple cider, sherry, etc.

Flavor makers:
artichoke bottoms, canned
artichoke hearts, marinated
bell peppers, roasted (in jars)
capers
chutney
crystallized ginger
dried mushrooms: shiitake, cremini, porcini, etc.
dried herbs and spices (garlic powder, curry powder, onion powder,
   oregano, chili powder, red pepper flakes, basil, etc.)
onion, dehydrated minced
hearts of palm, canned
mild and hot chiles, canned
nutritional yeast
salt-free seasoning blends (Mrs. Dash®, Herbamare®, etc.)
iodized sea salt and black pepper
jams and jellies (small jars)
sea vegetables: nori, dulse, wakame, kelp powder, etc.

sugar
sun-dried tomatoes
tapenade
vegetable bouillon cubes or powdered vegetable soup base
wasabi powder

Other:
baby food and supplies
pet food and supplies
aluminum foil
plastic film wrap
non-stick cooking spray
resealable food storage bags
vitamin C tablets and multi-vitamins

Note: When you make your shopping list, remember to add any special foods or ingredients that your family may require or prefer, including items for children and the elderly.

Going Global

When we lived in Hampton Roads, Virginia, we were privy to a sensational variety of international markets that included Asian, Indian, Middle Eastern, Italian, and Latino foods. If you don't already frequent such markets, schedule a shopping trip in search of the intriguing nonperishables listed below. These items are often less pricey than you will find at a natural food store, gourmet grocer, or supermarket.

In an Asian market, you might find such treats as wasabi peas, canned straw mushrooms, Thai curry mix, and dried shallots. An Italian market could yield instant polenta, small jars of cured olives, marinated vegetable salads, and canned

San Marzano tomatoes. Here is a partial list of food pantry items you might include in your.

Indian

Favorites: We love delicious protein-rich snack foods, such as dal-stuffed samosas. We also like the roasted chickpeas. There is an astonishing variety:

assorted vegetable and fruit chutneys
basmati rice pilaf mixes
golden fried onions
instant dosa mix (pancakes)
khari biscuits and other various biscuits and breads
panchrattan (potato and dried fruit mix)
roasted channa (chickpeas)
samosa snacks (stuffed with dal, cashews, raisins, and spices)
soya wadi (dehydrated soy chunks)
various pickled vegetables

Middle Eastern

Favorites: falafel mix (just add water) forms protein-rich veggie burgers. They're a great main dish. You can also shape falafel into small balls and fry them as a snack. Canned dolmas are almost as good as homemade.

bulgur
canned fava beans (ful medames)
dolmas
dried shallots and shallot powder
falafel mix
fried eggplant slices
pistachios
pita breads

Latino

Favorites: Plantain chips are a yummy snack and small cans of guava nectar make a nice change from OJ. You'll also find a good variety of canned beans and salsas. We especially enjoy the black refried beans served with plantain chips.

canned beans of all kinds
canned breadfruit nuts
guava spread
pickled cabbage
plantain chips
tropical fruit nectars
salsas in a variety of flavors and sizes
callaloo (a native vegetable stew)
canned zucchini flowers

Asian

Favorites: Canned or jarred wheat gluten is an easy way to get tasty chewy protein. It can be stir-fried or added to soups and stews. We also love the variety of canned mushrooms and roasted chestnuts.

curried vegetables and other flavors (shelf-stable 3-minute boil-in-bags)
canned mushrooms: oyster, golden needle, straw mushrooms
dried kanpyo (gourd strips)
noodle soups (ramen and beyond)
pickled vegetables (assorted)
canned vegetables: bamboo shoots, water chestnuts, bean sprouts, etc.
preserved yam candies (Asian gummy bears)
roasted chestnuts
wheat gluten and vegan mock meats
wasabi peas

Italian

Favorites: Caponata in a jar or can makes a wonderful snack (with crackers) or side dish. Other canned and jarred vegetables such as the roasted zucchini and giardiniera, taste great and make quick, easy, and flavorful veggie accompaniments for pasta dishes.

    antipasto salad
    caponata
    fava beans
    giardiniera
    gnocchi
    instant cups of risotto and more
    lupini beans
    marinated mushrooms
    roasted zucchini
    sliced eggplant strips

Keep Your Pantry List Handy

Be sure to save your Pantry Stash shopping list in a secure place to use down the road for filling in items you've pilfered from your stock. And remember: you can dip into your stock for more than just disasters and power outages. The nonperishables and recipes for them can be handy for first-time cooks, people who don't like to cook or don't know how, for efficiency apartment-dwellers, for moving to a new place before they connect the utilities, or extended road trips. In the next chapter, we'll move on to an essential requirement for Pantry Cuisine: a means of cooking without electricity.

Freeze-Dried Meals

You may discover occasions when you just don't feel like cooking, no matter how simple the recipes. For those times, there are "freeze dried" meals, which are generally available in pouches and require hot water to reconstitute them. Extremely lightweight, these foods are a favorite with hikers, backpackers, and campers. For vegan options, you'll have the best luck with PackLite Foods who make a few vegan freeze-dried and dehydrated meals (see contact info in the Resource Directory). Among their vegan offerings are Curry Lentil Soup, South of the Border Chili, and Minestrone. Freeze-dried meals can last for years if stored in a cool dry place.

If you choose to use them, it's important to know that they can be expensive: at $3.00-$6.00 each, buying enough to feed a family of four for a week can cost a fortune, though they're still cheaper than dining out in restaurants.

SRCs (Supermarket Ready-to-Cooks)

Sure, you could get by with prepared canned foods, but who wants to eat canned soups (notoriously high in salt) or spaghetti rings for even one meal much less a week. When you prepare your own Pantry Cuisine dishes with the recipes in this book, you can adjust those seasonings and ingredients according to your own taste. Yes, you'll be using canned ingredients, but it still beats prepared foods. In fact, we've found these recipes are very satisfying, especially when faced with life's little powerless challenges.

If you favor fresh foods in your diet, trips to the supermarket rarely include a trip down the packaged food aisle—you know, the one with the boxed "helpers" and packages of day-glow orange macaroni. Until we needed to load in supplies for our first hurricane, the canned food section was as esoteric to us as, well, canned foods. We figured as long as we had to eat pantry food, it should at least be as homemade as possible with as few preservatives, additives, and other ingredients we may not like. (What's your guess that a box that says "Italian-flavored" is not going to taste like it was prepared tableside by Mario Batali?)

Still, there is a place for a judicious amount of what I call "supermarket ready-to-cooks" (SRCs). Before you cast this book down in horror, you must allow the possibility of using these products. Some of them are heat-and-serve, while others require boiling water to reconstitute them. It's all about using your fuel judiciously. The next chapter explains your options for cooking SRCs as well as the recipes in this book.

To be ready for your next stretch without fresh foods, you would be well advised to stash a small supply of "instant packaged mixes," such as quick-cooking rice, instant oatmeal, instant soups, and even instant mashed potatoes. A few well-chosen SRCs can also serve to ease the workload of making dinner on an especially taxing day, satisfy fussy eaters in your family, and break up the routine. Having a few in the pantry can come in handy in a pinch. They're easy, economical, and a practical alternative when you don't feel like cooking.

Here are some examples of what I call SRCs:

Soups: available ready-to-eat in cans, jars, and aseptic boxes, as well as dehydrated in just-add-water envelopes and cups. If you buy the ubiquitous ramen noodle bricks, I recommend tossing out the "seasoning" packet before using, or look for healthier ramen varieties at natural food stores.

Pilafs: a wide range of quick-cooking rice, couscous, and other grain pilafs in a variety of flavors, including Cajun-style, Italian, Asian, and more.

Cereals: instant oatmeal, instant cream of wheat, instant grits.

Potatoes: instant mashed potatoes

Specialty foods: In my local supermarket I found canned Hoppin' John, Cajun rice and beans, chow-chow, and other savory side dishes. You can also find delicious Indian meals in shelf-stable packages from companies such as Jyoti,

Truly Indian, and Kitchens of India. Look for boxes of instant mixes including falafel, refried beans, risotto, taboulleh, sloppy joes, and other shelf-stable foods with many vegan selections from companies such as Eden Organic, Health Valley, Amy's, and Fantastic Foods.

READ LABELS CAREFULLY

Be sure to read labels carefully, as not all varieties of these products are vegan. Some brands kindly include a caveat in their labels that products were produced in the same facilities or with the same equipment where eggs or dairy are used.

When you shop for SRCs, be ready to read the fine print. If there are more than one or two words long enough to sabotage a Scrabble game, then you might want to leave it on the store shelf. In addition to well-stocked supermarkets, look for SRC candidates at natural food stores and international grocery stores. Keep in mind that many packaged foods are high in sodium and contain additives and preservatives. Seek out the healthiest ones you can find.

Yup: Baby Food

Even if you don't have babies, don't forget the value of baby food. Hear me out. Where else can you find small servings of not-too-bad tasting vegetables without additives? Sure, they'll need some help to perk up the flavor, but that's what herbs and spices are for. You can use pureed squash to make a creamy soup or sauce; try pureed plums for, well, a plum sauce; toss the pureed spinach with cooked grain or pasta and beans; use the bananas to make pancakes, and so on. To give baby food a test run, try the recipe for Spinach and White Bean Fritters on page 76.

Dehydrated Vegetables

When fresh vegetables are unavailable, dehydrated vegetables can come to the rescue. Among the virtues of dehydrated vegetables are that they taste better and cost less than canned. They also take up less space than canned, making them easier to store. In addition, dehydrated vegetables retain more nutritive value than canned or frozen vegetables and contain no sodium. A wide variety of vegetables are available in dehydrated form, including broccoli, cabbage, celery, corn, spinach, and potatoes.

Dehydrated vegetables easily rehydrate in water and most varieties double in volume when rehydrated. They are suggested as an alternative to canned vegetables in several of the recipes in this book. To use dehydrated vegetables in the recipes, simply measure out the required amount and rehydrate them in water before adding to the recipes. They can also be added to recipes in their dehydrated state, if enough additional water is added to rehydrate them while cooking. In addition to vegetables, you can also buy dehydrated (not dried) beans that cook up in 15 minutes. Several varieties of fruit are also available. We recommend Harmony House Foods (www.harmonyhousefoods.com) for dehydrated vegetables, beans, and fruits. They also carry freeze-dried ingredients. See Resources for details.

Do-It-Yourself Food Dehydration

Food dehydration has increased in popularity thanks to backpackers and raw food enthusiasts. In dehydration, the water is slowly removed and the food becomes lightweight and shelf-stable, thus making it ideal for emergency provisions. You can dehydrate any type of meal, even soups and stews or ingredients such as crackers, breads, vegetable chips, fruit leather, and cookies. During your day-to-day cooking routine, just make double recipes. Serve one for dinner and dehydrate the other for emergencies. Dehydrating is also a great way to have fresh produce at its nutritious peak and prepare it for future enjoyment without losing the nutrients.

You'll want to check out a book such as *Lip Smackin' Vegetarian Backpackin'* by Christine and Tim Conners (see Resources page 192), wherein the secrets to creating your own dehydrated meals are revealed, although some vegetarian recipes will need tweaking to make them vegan.

If you want to produce your own supply of fully prepared dehydrated meals, you'll need to invest in a food dehydrator. Roughly the size of a large microwave oven, a good dehydrator can set you back a couple of hundred bucks, but it can save money in the long run if you use it regularly.

MREs – Meals Ready to Eat

MREs ("meals ready-to-eat"), those individual meals sealed in retort packaging (tough plastic-laminated aluminum pouches) can be stored for months unrefrigerated. In a perfect world, MREs would be available for vegans, but the world isn't perfect, and though there are vegetarian MREs available, as of this writing, vegan MREs remain a mere twinkle in our vegan eye.

4

Making Fire

If you want to cook Pantry Cuisine in a non-emergency situation, you can do your cooking on your household stove with all the fresh vegetables you want. While the book offers several recipes that require no cooking at all (see page 56), when you're cooking without power, the single most important item for eating well is a reliable, safe, and efficient heat source.

Safety is of the utmost importance, as open flames pose an obvious danger to your home, family, and neighbors. Unless you have a working natural gas appliance available (and the authorities haven't turn off the gas), you'll want to consider the following advice for cooking, paying particular attention to the highly efficient and inexpensive single-burner butane stove.

Butane Stoves

For general home-based cooking, we recommend a single-burner butane unit like those that chefs use for cooking demos. The recipes in *Vegan Unplugged* were

The Glowmaster Portable
7000 BTU Stove

tested on a Glowmaster Portable Butane 7000 BTU stove, but several other brands, designed for both indoor and outdoor use, will work just as well. (Important: Make sure you buy a stove designed for indoor use.) In addition to using the stove to cook during emergency power outages, you can also use these stoves for camping, tailgate parties, boating, hot-pot cooking, and backyard cookouts. These stoves cost from $50 and up and can be found at restaurant supply stores and online. Fuel canisters are inexpensive and can be purchased with six or twelve to the case. (See the Resources Directory for more information.) Both stove and fuel canisters easily store in the back of a closet.

Gas Grills

We all know that gas grills work great for backyard barbecues, but if you have one with plenty of propane fuel, you can do all your cooking on it, weather and daylight permitting. Before a big hurricane strikes, it's a good idea to buy an extra tank of propane because the roads may be impassable for days. If the emergency is merely a blackout, for which you would have no warning, you shouldn't have trouble buying a tank of fuel anytime you need it. The downside to relying on a patio grill for all your cooking is that it can only be used outdoors. This is okay if it's warm and sunny but not too practical when it's cold, raining, or snowing outside, or when you just want to make a hot cup of tea before bed. Never use a gas grill inside your home or garage.

Camping Stoves

You may never have to reconstitute a dehydrated dinner while clinging to the side of Mt. Everest or while kayaking the North Sea, but if you pay a call to your nearest sporting goods chain or outfitter, you will discover an amazing array of portable cook stoves for the outdoors.

For about $50, you can have a tiny little stove and a canister of fuel that will last two days. These stoves are handy, but they're made mostly for backpacking and adventuring. Some of the stoves are little more than a tiny nozzle that sits atop a fuel canister. Using them will be frustrating if you want to heat a large skillet of food.

You can also check out the more efficient Coleman camp stoves. Coleman even makes a folding camp oven! Camp stoves often use white gas, naptha, or unleaded gasoline and are intended for outdoor use—never use them indoors. For indoor use, we recommend the butane stoves described on the previous page.

SOLAR COOKERS

Solar cookers employ the energy of the sun to cook food. The catch is, you need to have sunny weather, so this may not be the best option during an ice storm or rainy season. They work best in an equatorial climate.

Solar cookers can be expensive, but there are also ways to make a solar oven yourself. To check out solar cookers and ovens, go to the Gaiam website at www.gaiam.com.

Wood Fires

If you happen to have a wood-burning stove that allows you to cook on top, you can get by with this during a power outage, as long as you have a supply of wood that can last several days. If you're only using an open campfire, however, problems abound. It takes time to build a wood fire. Once the blaze starts, it doesn't heat uniformly. Also, much of the heat goes up in smoke. If you're outside or using an indoor fireplace, you will need to rig a way to heat a pot over the flames. For this, your pots and pans must have heatproof handles. Whenever you build a fire, use extreme caution.

Charcoal Grills

Charcoal is as impractical and inefficient for cooking as a wood fire. When you build a charcoal fire substantial enough for cooking, the charcoal will continue to burn long after you have eaten. You can't conserve charcoal very well or, of course, use it again. If you do use charcoal for boiling water, place a saucepan with the lid on the grill and cover if possible. Make sure you use a pan with heatproof handles. Unless you have a stockpile of dry charcoal, using this method will run you out of fuel in short order.

Microwave Modifications

Situations arise in which you may have electricity, but your only means of cooking is with a microwave, particularly if you live in a dorm or hotel room. Many of these recipes can be adapted to cook in your microwave, especially the "heat and serve" type dishes, such as Couscous Unplugged (page 100) and Ramen Fagiole (page 83). Just remember to use microwave-safe containers and microwave in short intervals, stopping to stir and check the food you are heating to make sure you don't overcook it.

Other Ways to Cook

With Sterno ("canned heat") or a chafing dish, you may not be able to boil enough water for pasta, but you will be able to warm up some soup. You can even heat cans of food on the manifold of your car engine, at least according to Chris Maynard and Bill Scheller who wrote a cookbook for "mechanic's cuisine" entitled, *Manifold Destiny: The One! The Only! Guide to Cooking on Your Car Engine.*

FIRE SAFETY PRECAUTIONS

Never burn charcoal or use any outdoor stove inside the house. Observe the utmost caution when using an open flame stove indoors. When cooking indoors, only use stoves specifically designed for indoor use. Also, never use candles indoors for light. Instead, use bona fide camping lights, safe oil lamps, or battery-operated lights.

- Place oil lamps safely away from flammable materials
- Keep children away from matches and open flames
- Keep an A-B-C fire extinguisher in your home
- Clear your cooking area of clutter
- Keep fittings and nozzles on bottled gas appliances clean
- Store bottled gas and other fuels away from heat sources
- Whenever cooking over open flames, be sure the cooking space is well ventilated

Other Equipment You'll Wish You Had

If you live in an area that's prone to a particular type of disaster, you have to face the possibility of one day having to get along without your blender, coffee grinder, and microwave. You may have to prepare meals manually with tools that don't whir, chop, or buzz, and for this, you'll need some basic manual kitchen tools.

For obvious reasons, you will also want to have a manual can opener. For prepping ingredients, you can probably get by with a sharp knife and potato masher, but other gadgets that can come in handy are a food mill for pureeing by hand and a box grater for shredding and grating. Whatever you use, be careful not to cut yourself. If you are in an emergency situation, the rescue squad may not be able to reach you, and blocked roads may prevent you from driving to a clinic or hospital. These hand-powered gadgets aren't essential for creating the recipes in this book, but they can come in handy whenever you experience a loss of power:

- can opener (manual)
- box grater
- food mill
- garlic press
- mortar and pestle
- nut grinder (hand crank)
- pastry blender
- potato masher or ricer
- strainers and sieves
- vegetable chopper (manual)
- vegetable peeler
- whisks

In the chapter that follows, we'll look at the innovative Pantry Cuisine, and show you how to transform canned or packaged ingredients into great-tasting meals whether you're in an emergency situation, on the road, or just don't feel like dealing with fresh food for supper. After that, it's on to the recipes.

5

Pantry Cuisine

Pantry Cuisine. Remember, you saw it here first.

During the years when Robin worked as a chef, I often had to fend for myself at mealtime. I never came anywhere close to her skills with food, but I learned how to make creative use of the pantry. So, when we began testing Pantry Cuisine recipes, even I found it easy, and if I can make these recipes, anyone can. The food tastes great, especially considering that it only uses nonperishables. It's a real lifesaver when you can't get fresh food. Pantry Cuisine is also quick and easy because it uses mostly one-pot cooking, cooks in 15 minutes or less, and is nutritionally balanced.

Recipes Unplugged

We all know "fresh is best" and that meals made from pantry ingredients aren't likely to measure up to meals made with fresh vegetables. However, when you are unplugged, whether by choice or necessity, especially for an extended period of time, these surprisingly delicious recipes will be your best option for great taste and high nutrition. This is achieved through the use of canned or dehydrated ingredients that you put up in your Pantry Stash.

We developed the recipes so you can cook them in 10 to 15 minutes to create maximum flavor while using minimum fuel. As an added bonus, most of the recipes were designed for one-pot cooking. This will make short work of both the cooking and the clean up. In order to economize on drinking water (you must also use precious fresh water to wash your dishes), some recipes will make double use of a single implement. For example, in making Pasta with White Beans and Olivada (page 87), you'll place the canned beans in a colander to drain, and then dump the cooked pasta over them. Since canned beans are precooked, the hot pasta water heats up the beans and rinses them at the same time.

GOT FRESH? USE FRESH.

In an emergency situation, you'll be using up your refrigerated and frozen foods within the first three days without power. During that time, feel free to substitute fresh vegetables in any of the recipes and use plugged-in stovetop cooking whenever it's available.

Included in the recipe chapters that follow are soups, stews, main dishes, salads, snacks, and desserts. They draw from your pantry and include all the recipes listed in the Five-Day Meal Box menus (Chapter 2). You won't need fancy equipment to make these recipes, only these basics:

1. a supply of ingredients from your Pantry Stash (Chapter 3)
2. a heat source, such as a single-burner butane stove (Chapter 4)

3. pots, pans, and cooking utensils
4. enough potable water for cooking

The book also includes nineteen recipes that require no cooking at all. (See page 56.) The No-Cook recipes are indicated by this icon:

The Harder the Veggie, the Longer They Cook

Our ancestors stored onions, garlic, potatoes, squashes, and root vegetables, such as carrots and parsnips, in cool, dry root cellars. Today's houses are more likely to have a wine cellar than a root cellar, but that doesn't mean you can't store root veggies there (or another cool dry place). These sturdy vegetables can tolerate sitting around at room temperature for several days or longer, and, in fact, you may already be storing them at room temperature. However, don't forget that cooking them uses a lot of fuel.

This means, you'd better put off that glorious bisque you'd been planning to make with a magnificent five-pound kabocha squash. Instead, open a can of pumpkin puree and make Curried-Spice Pumpkin Bisque (page 129). This tasty soup will be ready in minutes, instead of hours, and you'll have enough fuel left to make many more meals.

Onion Strategies

The same goes for cooking fresh onions versus dehydrated ones. You'll need to tack on an extra five minutes or so of cooking time to soften a chopped onion—double for carrots. If you do plan to use fresh onions, be sure to use small ones, because you can't have the leftover half of a large one sitting around until tomorrow. As an option, consider switching to shallots. These delicate beauties are small, cook fast, and can add a touch of elegance to your masterpiece vegan slumgullion. Plus, did you know that the shallot is the only member of the onion family that doesn't give you "the breath from hell"? In ancient times, shallots were considered an aphrodisiac, perhaps for that reason.

Why No Potatoes?

Even though onions, potatoes, and a few other fresh produce items can be stored without refrigeration, they are not included in the Pantry Stash because they take longer to cook. As in most situations without electricity, you may have limited fuel, so waiting 10 minutes for, say, potatoes to soften may be a luxury you can't afford.

If fuel is not an issue, and you have fresh produce on hand, by all means use them instead of the dehydrated or canned versions called for in the recipes. It's really a matter of common sense—if you have fresh produce, use it. If not, you'll be glad you have Pantry Cuisine options.

Garlic, Lemons, and Ginger Are Your Friends

When you're unplugged for a length of time, garlic can be your best friend because it prefers room temperature. Not only is garlic shelf-stable, it also cooks quickly. Garlic adds tons of flavor to whatever you're cooking, so it's great to use in these recipes.

Some of the recipes call for two "borderline" shelf-stable ingredients: lemon (and lime) juice and ginger. Fresh lemon juice can perk up foods in magical ways, so if you know a storm is brewing, buy a few fresh lemons. Although inferior to fresh juice, you can also keep one of those little plastic lemons containing reconstituted lemon juice on hand. These recipes call for "lemon juice"—so use whichever you have. Ditto for limes and lime juice.

Fresh ginger is an optional ingredient in some of the recipes. It's a rhizome that tolerates room temperature quite well until it's been cut. The incomparable flavor of fresh ginger when added to certain dishes makes it worth keeping handy. Once you slice or grate a portion of gingerroot, wrap what's left tightly in plastic. It won't keep as long, but you can use it for a day or two by slicing off and discarding the cut portion before using it again.

You can also buy in advance some underripe bananas, avocados, pears, and tomatoes, as they can ripen unrefrigerated on the windowsill to provide fresh nutrients down the road. Beyond lemons and limes, other citrus fruits such as oranges and grapefruits also do well at room temperature.

If you stocked your Pantry Stash, you will be prepared for cooking meals under powerless conditions. If you do have some fresh produce to incorporate into these recipes, then by all means use it while it lasts. If you have fresh herbs, feel free to substitute fresh for dried (1 teaspoon of dried = 1 tablespoon of fresh). The most important thing with these recipes is to be creative and have fun modifying them to suit your needs and tastes.

The Fridge

Let us begin by determining what needs to be cooked first. Cold temperatures preserve food, whether refrigerated or frozen, but if you're experiencing a power outage, your stored cold foods will begin to defrost and spoil. Your first meals during a power outage, therefore, will use up what's in the refrigerator first, followed by what's in the freezer. Use them in this order:

1. anything highly perishable (leftovers or other home-cooked foods, open "refrigerate after opening" containers, refrigerated tofu or soy milk)
2. moderately perishable items such as leafy greens
3. items that may last longer, such as firm, hard, or uncut vegetables

Before you start using up the perishables, make a list of what you have on hand

and separate the items into workable menus. I don't know about your fridge, but in ours, at any given time you might find truffle oil, jicama, arugula, umeboshi plums, maitake mushrooms, three kinds of tofu, and fresh fennel. Since everyone will have different perishables on hand, it's not possible to provide you with menus for using them up. However, I can share the following story to illustrate the point.

In anticipation of Hurricane Isabel, we purchased only nonperishables at the supermarket that week and used up as much of the perishable "good stuff" in the days preceding the storm. The first day without power, our refrigerator still offered a few carrots, some celery, scallions, fresh parsley, and green beans. A container of previously cooked escarole and several very ripe tomatoes from our garden were also prime candidates for the cook pot. Of course, we also had onions and garlic. So how did we fare?

The first meal after Isabel, we cooked Italian. For lunch, we made a small pot of soup with fresh vegetables, adding the cooked escarole close to serving time. With the nearly overripe tomatoes, we made a puttanesca sauce (page 85) for dinner, which also allowed us to use up the remaining parsley and a partial container of imported olives that languished on the refrigerator shelf. With no food processor, we did the chopping by hand: each with a small cutting board and a couple of sharp Henkels', tapping our feet to the beat of the hand-crank radio. We took our time. We had no place to go and needed ways to keep occupied. An

> ## SODIUM WATCH
>
> Many canned and packaged foods are high in sodium, so you may want to use less salt when you cook. That's where salt-free and low-sodium seasoning blends can help. Salt-free blends, such as Mrs. Dash, come in a variety of flavors from lemon pepper to spicy Cajun. Natural food stores offer organic seasonings, such as Herbamare, a blend of herbs and sea salt, which is lower in sodium than table salt. **NOTE:** Be sure to use iodized sea salt whenever possible.

hour after enjoying the last twirl of pasta, we remembered several ripe peaches, which led to an inspired dessert. And so it was, that, instead of feeling sorry for ourselves, we spent our time creating a fabulous meal that would have been delicious even with electrical power.

So, make meals that are appetizing, nutritious, and easy—limited only by what you have on hand and your imagination. Be creative, and try to incorporate a theme of some sort to tie the meal together. Successive meals would be similarly planned to use up what's in your refrigerator. If you have to cook a lot of food to save it from the garbage can, go ahead and make a mountainous stir-fry. You can also grill everything in sight in a backyard cookout. If all you have are small amounts of miscellaneous vegetables, make a soup or stew. If you're truly well-stocked, share the bounty. Invite neighbors over. If you know of an elderly couple down the street, bring them some portions of whatever you make. They'll be thrilled for the hot meal and think of you fondly when the big mess is over.

By the second day without power, your refrigerator should be bare of most perishable foods. Leafy produce generally wilts beyond the point of salvaging. It's okay to keep some of the condiments in there that don't spoil easily, such as soy sauce, ketchup, and mustard. For a recipe that can help you use up your fresh veggies, see the recipe for Rosemary-Scented Bricolage on page 53.

FOOD TEMPERATURE SAFETY

According to the USDA, when food is stored above 40 degrees F., bacteria can double every 20 minutes. This is true of raw foods as well as cooked foods. Foods in a jammed, well-insulated freezer stay frozen longest, up to three days, if the door remains closed. The presence of ice crystals in the center of food tells you that a frozen item is safe to eat. Use caution—if it's thawed, don't risk it. (See page 171.) Only open the refrigerator and freezer doors when absolutely necessary.

The Freezer

You used up the fridge fodder first, because it spoils first. Now it's time to raid the freezer and cook all those items that you must either use or lose. The same basic rules apply as on Day One. Cook as much of the "good stuff" as your family, friends, and neighbors can reasonably eat. Once your freezer items have completely thawed, either cook them, give them away, or toss them.

Logic tells us to cook the most expensive stuff first, sacrificing the cheaper items, if necessary. Keep in mind that, depending on the reason for the power outage and your insurance coverage, the loss of the contents of your fridge and freezer may be covered by your insurance policy—so, be sure to run a tab as you throw things out.

The day after Isabel, the skies were clear and blue, and virtually everyone with an outdoor grill was cooking outside, so we cooked a good old-fashioned American BBQ with vegan burgers, seitan, and a grilled vegetable feast. Whether your grill sizzles with vegan burgers, portobello mushroom caps, or skewered vegetables, this is the time when grilling out becomes more of a necessity than a whim. If at all possible, try to immerse yourself in the "fun" of a cookout and forget the work and the waiting that still lies ahead.

> ## THE MAGIC OF HERBS
>
> "A man can live on packaged food from here til Judgment Day, if he's got enough rosemary."
>
> —Shepherd Book *(Serenity)*

Even during emergency cooking, you will want to pay attention to basic nutritional guidelines. Whenever possible, be sure to include beans, nuts, or other protein and a variety of vegetables and fruit. Disasters sometimes dictate what you can eat, but if you have prepared your pantry well, you should still have lots of flexibility.

A Recipe for the Last of Your Fresh Veggies

This recipe is designed to use up any fresh or frozen ingredients that you may have on hand. When cooking hard root veggies, conserve fuel by cutting them as thin as possible so they cook faster. If you're missing an ingredient, double up on what you have or substitute another.

Rosemary-Scented Bricolage

Call it a "stew made from odds and ends," and no one rushes to the table. But call it "bricolage," and you'll have them eating out of your hand.

1. Heat the oil in a large saucepan over medium heat. Add the onion, garlic, potatoes, carrots, and rosemary. Cover and cook, stirring occasionally, until vegetables soften.

2. Add the cabbage, beans, broth, and salt and pepper to taste, and bring to a boil. Reduce heat, cover, and simmer until vegetables are tender, about 15 minutes. Adjust seasonings.

MAKES 4 SERVINGS

- 1 tablespoon olive oil
- 1 yellow onion, finely chopped
- 3 garlic cloves, minced
- 2 potatoes, cut into 1/4-inch dice
- 2 carrots, thinly sliced
- 2 teaspoons fresh rosemary or 1 teaspoon dried
- 1/2 small head cabbage, finely shredded
- 1 (15.5-ounce) can white beans, drained
- 1 1/2 cups vegetable broth (see page 119)
- Salt and black pepper

Things You Should Know About the Recipes

The next five chapters contain eighty Pantry Cuisine recipes that have been designed for simple and speedy preparation. Why simple and why speedy? Because, whether you're on the road or stuck at home waiting for the electricity to be restored, you will need to conserve your cooking (drinkable) water and fuel. Pantry Cuisine is about extending your resources as far as possible, so you need to be familiar with the universe you are entering.

Preparing the recipes in this book have some things in common that you need to know about:

1. The recipes presume that you have used up your fresh and frozen foods and are now relying on your pantry items. Most of the recipes can accommodate the inclusion of fresh vegetables, as long as they can be cooked quickly (usually by slicing thinly) so as not to waste fuel.

2. Since you will probably be using a single burner stove, you can only prepare one course at a time. Of course, salads, some desserts, and snacks, which require no heat, can be served with the hot soups, stews, or entrees. Otherwise, cook and eat the heated recipes in separate courses.

3. Most of the recipes make 4 servings, depending on how much you eat. They are easily doubled. Since you can't store leftovers, it's better to prepare less than more.

4. Recipes calling for non-dairy milk assume that you will be using either shelf-stable aseptic containers of soy or rice milk or reconstituting a powdered mix. The trick is to reconstitute only as much of the powdered variety as you need. After you open an aseptic container, be sure to finish it in one sitting, as it won't be safe to drink by the next day once opened.

With your temporary dining universe now defined, try to think "conservation" each time you cook. One way to do this is to observe the *mise en place* concept used in professional kitchens. The phrase literally means to "put in place," and involves setting up all the ingredients you will need to make the meal. Pre-measure everything and place it conveniently near your burner before you turn on the gas.

Now You're Cooking

These recipes can be cooked in a variety of ways, but the instructions and cooking times are intended for the single-burner butane stove. There are nineteen recipes that require no cooking at all! (See page 56.) A case of extra fuel cans provides enough fuel to keep us cooking for a few weeks. As a back-up and for variety, we also have an outdoor gas grill, a chafing dish, a fondue pot, and a box of Sterno cans. In general, we've gotten by nicely using the butane cooker for most cooking and the outdoor grill for, well, grilling.

Vegetable Grilling for the Common Man

As discussed above, when the power goes out, the first things you cook should be perishable foods from your refrigerator, including fresh vegetables. For these, you can use your outdoor grill.

Grilling vegetables over a flame caramelizes their natural sugars and intensifies the flavors. So go ahead and grill your bell peppers, eggplant, portobello mushrooms, and fennel bulbs. Cut them into uniform pieces, brush them with olive oil, soak them in a marinade, or rub them with a spice blend, and place the pieces on the grill. The vegetables can also be threaded onto wooden or metal skewers, and served over pasta or rice. If you don't feel like cleaning a grill, cut-up the veggies, douse with seasonings or a marinade or spice rub and seal in portion-sized envelopes of heavy-duty aluminum foil.

The "No Cook" Recipe List

While many of the recipes in this book require short cooking times, several require no cooking at all. Below is a handy list of the "no-cook" recipes, which are also marked within the recipe chapters by the helpful No-Cook icon pictured above.

Texturized Soy Protein and Soy Curls

When you're unplugged, perishable ingredients such as tempeh, seitan, and tofu won't do you much good. That's where shelf-stable dehydrated products such as texturized soy protein and Soy Curls can come to your rescue. Just soak in hot water for 10 minutes to reconstitute, and you've got a protein-dense main ingredient that you only need to heat up for a few minutes.

Texturized soy protein (also known as texturized vegetable protein or TVP) is made from defatted soy flour and is available in two forms: granular and chunky. A great source of protein, texturized soy protein absorbs flavors well and brings a "meaty" texture to dishes. You can find it in well-stocked supermarkets and natural food stores. It is also available online. The granular-style texturized soy protein can be used to make great chili and tacos or as an addition to spaghetti sauce. The chunky version is good in stews, soups, and stir-fries and can be used instead of beans in many of the recipes in this book: simply place the about 1 cup of texturized soy protein in a heatproof bowl (large enough to allow for expansion) and add enough hot water to cover. Then drain and add to recipes.

Soy Curls, made by Butler Foods, is another dehydrated vegan meat alternative. They have a great texture, are extremely versatile, and can be used to make fajitas, sandwiches, stir-fries and more. Available in some stores and online, one (8-ounce) package contains approximately 4 1/2 cups of Soy Curls. Like texturized soy protein, Soy Curls must be soaked in hot water for 10 minutes to reconstitute. For more information, visit: www.butlerfoods.com.

About Non-Dairy Milks

Many brands and varieties of non-dairy milk, including soy, rice, almond, and oat, are available in shelf-stable aseptic containers that need no refrigeration until they are opened. The 1-quart containers, however, need to be used up quickly, unless you can keep the open container on ice. For smaller portions, look for soy milk and rice milk in great little 8-ounce aseptic boxes—the perfect amount to use in most recipes. Soy milk and rice milk are also available in a dry powder form that can be reconstituted as needed with water. The recipes in this book can be made with either. Another dairy-free milk option for certain recipes is unsweetened coconut milk, which is available in 13-ounce cans.

● ● ●

You don't have to wait for a disaster to get your money's worth out of *Vegan Unplugged*. If you like to cook with pantry ingredients, you won't find a cookbook anywhere that provides the versatility, variety, and nutrition in meals that take under fifteen minutes to prepare.

LEMONS AND LIMES

Sailors know that whole lemons and limes last for weeks without refrigeration if tightly wrapped in foil.

6

Bean and Vegetable Main Dishes

Even if you secretly delight in an occasional plain can of beans, no one likes having to eat the same food every day. This chapter provides a variety of tasty main courses that feature canned beans and canned or dehydrated vegetables from your Pantry Stash. When you want to convert cupboard stuff into delicious meals, these are the recipes that can do it. They taste good and are packed with nutrients to give you and your family ample protein, vitamins, and minerals. With your trusty butane burner, you will transform your supply of pantry goods into luscious dishes such as Moroccan-Spiced Vegetable Stew, Polenta Fiesta, and Beat-the-Blahs Black Bean Patties.

Bean and Vegetable Main Dishes

Samosadillas

Quick Bean Burritos

Old Bay Chickpea Cakes

Garlicky Chickpeas with Potatoes and Tomatoes

Almost-Instant Black Bean Chili

Red Rum Chili

Moroccan-Spiced Vegetable Stew

Polenta Fiesta

"Great Personality" Hash

Beat-the-Blahs Black Bean Patties

Curry in a Hurry

Tuscan Chickpea Stew

Thaiphoon Tofu Stir-Fry

Spinach and White Bean Fritters

High-Water Hoppin' John

Samosadillas

Food cravings can come at the darnedest times, like when your kitchen is unplugged. It was that way for us with samosas. Armed with shelf-stable flour tortillas and our well-stocked pantry, we whipped up these samosa-quesadilla hybrids in minutes. Craving satisfied. **Note:** If you don't have chutney, make a chutney "do-fer" by combining 1/3 cup of peach jam with a tablespoon of cider vinegar, some raisins, red pepper flakes, and grated ginger.

1. Place the potatoes in a saucepan and mash them with a potato masher or ricer. Add the peas, chiles, raisins, soy sauce, curry powder, coriander, cumin, chili powder, and salt and pepper to taste. Mix well and heat over medium heat until hot, stirring as needed, about 5 minutes.

2. Cut the tortillas into quarters. Spoon about 2 tablespoons of the filling onto each piece of tortilla. Fold one side over the filling and press lightly to flatten. Set aside. Repeat with the remaining ingredients.

3. Arrange the samosadillas in a nonstick skillet over medium heat. Cook until lightly browned and heated through, turning once, about 8 minutes total. Serve hot with chutney.

MAKES 4 SERVINGS

1 (16-ounce) can white potatoes, drained or 3/4 cup dehydrated potatoes, rehydrated (page 34)
1 (4-ounce) can green peas, drained or 1/4 cup dehydrated peas, rehydrated (page 34)
1 (4-ounce) can hot or mild diced green chiles, drained
2 tablespoons raisins
1 tablespoon soy sauce
1 tablespoon curry powder
2 teaspoons ground coriander
1 teaspoon ground cumin
1 teaspoon chili powder
Salt and black pepper
4 flour tortillas
1 small jar chutney

Quick Bean Burritos

These burritos taste great and couldn't be easier to make. They are a satisfying lunch, even when you're plugged in.

1 (15.5-ounce) can pinto beans, drained
2 teaspoons chili powder
1 cup tomato salsa
1 (4-ounce) can chopped mild green chiles, drained
4 large flour tortillas

1. Combine the beans and chili powder in a saucepan and mash the beans well. Add the salsa and chiles. Stir to combine. Cook over medium heat until hot, adding a little water if the mixture begins to stick to the pan.

2. To serve, divide the bean mixture among the tortillas and roll up. Serve hot.

MAKES 4 SERVINGS

CONDIMENTS ON ICE

If you stock up on ice before a storm, you can use it to keep some prepared foods chilled, stretch the life of your condiments, and hold leftovers for another meal. Even without ice, acidic condiments, such as soy sauce, mustard, and ketchup will still be safe for several days.

Old Bay Chickpea Cakes

Zesty seasonings have a transformative effect on a can of chickpeas in these flavorful crisply fried cakes. They're reminiscent of crab cakes, but in a good way.

1. Place the chickpeas in a medium bowl and mash well. Add the remaining ingredients except the bread crumbs and oil. Mix until well combined.

2. Pour the breadcrumbs into a shallow bowl. Shape the mixture into 8 small patties and dredge in the breadcrumbs.

3. Heat the oil in a large skillet over medium heat. Add the patties, in batches if needed, and cook until browned on both sides, turning once. Serve hot.

MAKES 4 SERVINGS

1 (15.5-ounce) can chickpeas, drained and mashed
1/4 cup wheat gluten flour (vital wheat gluten)
3 tablespoons nutritional yeast
2 teaspoons kelp powder
1 tablespoon lemon juice
1 teaspoon Old Bay Seasoning
1/2 teaspoon garlic powder
1/2 teaspoon onion powder
1/2 teaspoon dry mustard
1/4 teaspoon cayenne
Salt and black pepper
1/2 cup dried breadcrumbs
Olive oil, for frying

When You're Plugged In:
Recipe Upgrades

These recipes are adaptable for everyday cooking when the power is on, including cooking at home, on the road, or at school. In such cases, you can "upgrade" the recipes. Here are some examples:

1. You have fresh produce: If you have fresh vegetables, fruits, and other perishable ingredients, substitute them in any of the recipes.

2. Fresh water is available: If you don't need to ration your water, then go ahead and rinse your canned beans.

3. Unlimited cooking fuel: If you have plenty of fuel for cooking, put on that pot of water to cook up some of the longer-cooking pastas, grains, and vegetables.

4. You've got a mini-fridge: If you're plugged in, but are limited to a mini-fridge (i.e., efficiency apartment; hotel room; college dorm; etc.), you can use that tiny space for ingredients to upgrade the recipes such as soy products, seitan, and fresh produce.

When You're Unplugged:
Worst-Case-Scenario Recipes

The pantry-ingredient recipes in this book were developed for worst-case-scenario conditions in which you have no power or refrigeration. They share the following assumptions:

1. You are unplugged: No electricity, no refrigeration, no electric stove or oven, no microwave, and no food processor or blender.

2. No perishables available: Fresh foods are used up and unavailable. The only ingredients you have are non-perishable pantry ingredients.

3. Limited fuel for heat: The only heat source available for cooking is a single-burner butane stove, a camp stove, gas grill, or wood stove. For this reason, the recipe cooking times are limited to no more than 10 or 15 minutes to conserve fuel.

4. Limited water: Fresh water for washing pans and dishes may be in short supply. Whenever possible, you'll cook these recipes in a single pan or pot so clean-up conserves water.

Garlicky Chickpeas with Potatoes and Tomatoes

Canned chickpeas combine with diced canned potatoes and tomatoes for a flavorful meal seasoned with garlic, herbs, and olive oil. Like other recipes in this book, you can prepare this recipe using virtually any heat source that can accommodate a saucepan or skillet. For a complete one-dish meal, add canned or dehydrated spinach or fresh cooked greens.

1 tablespoon olive oil
3 garlic cloves, minced
1 teaspoon dried basil
1/2 teaspoon dried savory
1/4 teaspoon red pepper flakes
1 (16-ounce) can white potatoes, drained and diced
1 (15.5-ounce) can chickpeas, drained
1 (14.5-ounce) can diced tomatoes, drained
Salt and black pepper

1. Heat the oil in a large saucepan or skillet over medium heat. Add the garlic, basil, savory, and red pepper flakes, if using, and cook until fragrant, about 30 seconds.

2. Stir in the potatoes, chickpeas, tomatoes, and salt and pepper to taste. Cover and cook until the flavors are blended and the tomatoes break up somewhat and become saucy, about 10 minutes.

MAKES 4 SERVINGS

Almost-Instant Black Bean Chili

This hearty chili is made with canned beans and a jar of salsa. Cook it over any heat source, just long enough to heat through and marry the flavors. Serve over quick-cooking rice or noodles, or eat it plain right out of the pot.

1. If using texturized soy protein, place it in a heatproof bowl with enough hot water to cover and set aside for 10 minutes to reconstitute. Combine the ingredients (including the reconstituted texturized soy protein, if using) in a saucepan, reserving half the corn. Cover and cook over moderate heat, stirring occasionally. Add as much water as needed to create a sauce and prevent sticking to the bottom of the pan.

2. Reduce heat to medium and simmer, stirring frequently, until heated through and long enough to cook off any raw taste from the chili powder, about 15 minutes. Garnish with the remaining corn kernels.

MAKES 4 SERVINGS

1/2 cup texturized soy protein granules (optional)

2 (15.5-ounce) cans black beans, drained

1 (16-ounce) jar salsa (hot or mild)

2 to 3 tablespoons chili powder, or to taste

1 tablespoon dehydrated minced onion

1 (15-ounce) can corn kernels, drained or 1/3 cup dehydrated corn kernels, rehydrated (page 34)

1 cup water, or as needed

Red Rum Chili

Dark red kidney beans and a shot of dark rum. Yum. Yeah, this chili will put hair on your chest. To make it heartier, add some reconstituted texturized soy protein. Serve with crackers or ladle it over rice or noodles. NOTE: If you already used up your last drop of rum in a batch of Mai Tais, just leave it out.

1/2 cup texturized soy protein granules (optional)
1 tablespoon olive oil
2 to 3 tablespoons chili powder
1 (15-ounce) can crushed tomatoes
1 (14.5-ounce) can diced tomatoes, undrained
2 tablespoons dehydrated minced onion
2 tablespoons dark rum
1 (4-ounce) can mild or hot chopped green chiles, drained
2 (15.5-ounce) cans kidney beans, drained
Salt and black pepper

1. If using texturized soy protein, place it in a heatproof bowl with enough hot water to cover and set aside for 10 minutes to reconstitute. Heat the oil in a large saucepan over medium heat. Stir in the chili powder, tomatoes, onions, and rum, stirring to blend.

2. Add the chiles, beans, reconstituted texturized soy protein, if using, and salt and pepper to taste. Bring to a boil. Reduce heat to low and simmer, stirring occasionally, until flavors are blended, about 15 minutes. Taste to adjust seasonings. Serve hot.

MAKES 4 SERVINGS

Moroccan-Spiced Vegetable Stew

Fragrant spices and dried fruits lend a Moroccan flavor to this hearty stew that just begs to be served over couscous. You can make some instant couscous first and cover it to keep it warm until the stew is ready.

1. Place the dried fruit and raisins or currants in a small heatproof bowl. Add enough boiling water to cover and soak for 15 minutes to soften.

2. In a large saucepan, heat the oil over medium heat. Add the garlic, cumin, and cinnamon and cook, stirring, for 30 seconds. Add the tomatoes, chickpeas, onion, and broth and bring to a boil.

3. Reduce heat to low, add the green beans, carrots, and reserved fruit. Season to taste with salt and pepper.

4. Simmer, stirring occasionally, until flavors are blended and the desired consistency is reached, about 10 minutes.

MAKES 4 SERVINGS

1/2 cup dried mixed fruit
1/4 cup raisins or currants
1 tablespoon olive oil
2 garlic cloves, minced
1 teaspoon ground cumin
1 teaspoon ground cinnamon
1 (14.5-ounce) can diced tomatoes, drained
1 (15.5-ounce) can chickpeas, drained
1 tablespoon dehydrated minced onion
1 1/4 cups vegetable broth (page 119)
1 (15-ounce) can green beans, drained or 3/4 cup dehydrated green beans, rehydrated (page 34)
1 (8-ounce) can sliced carrots, drained or 1/3 cup dehydrated carrots, rehydrated (page 34)
Salt and black pepper

Polenta Fiesta

In the store, look for either instant polenta or shelf-stable vacuum-sealed packages. If you're using an instant polenta mix, prepare the polenta first and then proceed with the recipe.

1 package pre-cooked polenta, cut into 1/2-inch slices

1 tablespoon olive oil

1 (14-ounce) jar hot or mild tomato salsa

1 (15.5-ounce) can pinto beans, drained

1 (8-ounce) can corn kernels, drained or 1/3 cup dehydrated corn, rehydrated (page 34)

1 (4-ounce) can chopped mild chiles, drained

1 teaspoon chili powder

1/2 teaspoon onion powder

Salt and black pepper

1. Pan-fry the polenta slices in the olive oil in a hot skillet until browned on both sides. Alternately, brush the polenta slices with the olive oil and grill them on a hot grill. Set aside to keep warm.

2. In a saucepan, combine the remaining ingredients and heat until hot and the flavors are well combined. Spoon the salsa mixture over the polenta and serve.

MAKES 4 SERVINGS

CAN SIZES

Recipes often call for specific can sizes, but you don't have to be a stickler. If a recipe calls for a 15.5-ounce can, and you have a 16-ouncer, the results will be the same.

"Great Personality" Hash

Right. It's not much to look at, but it has great personality. This tasty dish is hard to stop eating once you start. Blot the ingredients before adding to the skillet, and the hash will develop a crispy brown outer crust. Slather with ketchup, of course, but use Herbamare, Mrs. Dash, or some other seasoning blend, instead of salt, as some of the ingredients already contain salt (See Sodium Watch on page 50).

1. Heat the oil in large skillet over medium-high heat. Mash the potatoes a bit to break up and add to the skillet along with the roasted red bell pepper, lentils, and peas.

2. Drizzle with the soy sauce and sprinkle with the onion powder. Season with salt-free seasoning blend and pepper to taste. Cook until hot and slightly browned on outside, turning frequently with spatula, about 10 minutes total.

MAKES 4 SERVINGS

1 tablespoon olive oil
1 (15-ounce) can diced potatoes, drained and blotted
1 (7-ounce) jar roasted red bell peppers, chopped and blotted
1 (15.5-ounce) can cooked lentils or kidney beans, drained and mashed
1 (8-ounce) can green peas or 1/3 cup dehydrated green peas, rehydrated (page 34), drained and mashed
1 tablespoon soy sauce
1/2 teaspoon onion powder
Low-sodium seasoning blend (Herbamare, Mrs. Dash, etc.)
Black pepper

Beat-the-Blahs Black Bean Patties

These incredibly tasty patties can be served with a variety of sauces. It all depends on what flavor you're craving. Spicy peanut sauce works great, and so does salsa or barbecue sauce.

1 (15-ounce) can diced white
  potatoes, drained
1 (15.5-ounce) can black beans,
  drained
1 tablespoon dehydrated minced
  onion
1 teaspoon dried parsley
3/4 cup dried breadcrumbs
Salt and black pepper
1 tablespoon olive oil

1. In a large bowl, mash the potatoes and beans with a potato ricer until well mashed. Add the onion, parsley, breadcrumbs, and salt and pepper, to taste. Mix until well combined.

2. Divide the mixture into 6 equal portions and use your hands to shape into patties.

3. Heat the oil in a large skillet over medium heat. Cook the bean patties until golden brown on both sides, about 5 minutes per side. Drain on paper towels and serve hot with your favorite sauce.

MAKES 6 PATTIES

Curry in a Hurry

No doubt about it, this curry is best served over rice. If you only have one cooking flame, make the rice first, cover, and set it on the side until you make the curry. The rice will retain much of its heat, because this curry goes together so quickly that the rice doesn't have a chance to cool.

1. Heat the oil in a large saucepan over medium heat. Stir in the curry powder and cook until fragrant, 30 seconds. Blend in the broth.

2. Add the kidney beans, carrots, potatoes, tomatoes, chiles, and onion, and bring to a boil.

3. Reduce the heat to low, and season with salt and pepper to taste. Simmer for 10 minutes to blend the flavors.

MAKES 4 SERVINGS

2 teaspoons olive oil
2 tablespoons curry powder
1 1/4 cups vegetable broth (see page 119)
1 (15.5-ounce) can dark red kidney beans, drained
1 (15-ounce) can sliced carrots, drained, or 3/4 cup dehydrated carrots, rehydrated (page 34)
1 (15-ounce) can sliced potatoes, drained
1 (14.5-ounce) can diced tomatoes, drained
1 (4-ounce) can chopped mild chiles, drained
1 tablespoon dehydrated minced onion
Salt and black pepper

Tuscan Chickpea Stew

During an extended power outage, you may wish that you were someplace else. As long as you're wishing, why not pretend you're enjoying this Tuscan-inspired stew in the courtyard of an Italian villa.

2 teaspoons olive oil
2 garlic cloves, minced
1/4 cup dry white wine
1/2 teaspoon dried marjoram
2 (15.5-ounce) cans chickpeas, drained
1 (15-ounce) can sliced white potatoes, drained
1 (15-ounce) can artichoke hearts, drained and chopped
1 (6-ounce) jar roasted red bell pepper, drained and chopped
1 tablespoon dehydrated minced onion
1 bay leaf
1 1/4 cups vegetable broth (see page 119)
Salt and black pepper

1. Heat the oil in a large saucepan over medium heat. Add the garlic and cook until fragrant, 30 seconds. Stir in the wine and marjoram.

2. Add the chickpeas, potatoes, artichoke hearts, bell peppers, onion, and bay leaf.

3. Stir in the broth and bring to a boil. Reduce the heat to low, season with salt and pepper to taste, and simmer to develop the flavors, about 10 minutes. Remove the bay leaf before serving.

MAKES 4 SERVINGS

RINSE BEANS WHEN POSSIBLE

Canned beans are usually rinsed under cold water, but if your taps are dry, you won't want to waste water rinsing beans. Beans are okay to eat unrinsed. Just remember, if the water is flowing, rinse your beans.

Thaiphoon Tofu Stir-Fry

If you like Thai flavors, try this stir-fry. Feel free to substitute any fresh ingredients you have on hand. It's great even if you don't have fresh ginger.

1. Prepare the rice according to package directions. Set aside.

2. Heat the oil in a large skillet or wok over medium-high heat. Add the garlic, ginger (if using), tofu, red pepper, and sugar, and stir-fry until the tofu is golden brown.

3. Add the soy sauce, mushrooms, Chinese vegetables, and chiles, and stir-fry until hot.

4. Serve over the rice, sprinkled with the peanuts.

MAKES 4 SERVINGS

NOTE: Reconstituted Soy Curls or texturized soy protein chunks can be substituted for the tofu in this recipe.

1 cup quick-cooking rice
1 tablespoon canola oil
2 garlic cloves, minced
2 teaspoons grated fresh ginger (optional)
1 (12-ounce) box extra-firm silken tofu, drained and patted dry, cut into 1/2-inch dice
1/2 teaspoon red pepper flakes, or to taste
1/2 teaspoon sugar
2 tablespoons soy sauce
1 (15-ounce) can straw mushrooms, drained
1 (15-ounce) can Chinese vegetables, drained
1 (4-ounce) can chopped mild chiles, drained
1/4 cup dry-roasted peanuts

Spinach and White Bean Fritters

With no additives and a rich spinach flavor, a jar of spinach baby food is the secret ingredient to these tasty protein-rich fritters. Any other kind of cooked spinach can be used in this recipe, including fresh, frozen, rehydrated, or canned.

1 (15.5-ounce) can white beans, drained
1 (4-ounce) jar spinach baby food
2 tablespoons lemon juice
1/4 cup ground walnuts
3 tablespoons dried breadcrumbs
3 tablespoons all-purpose flour
1 teaspoon baking powder
1/2 teaspoon onion powder
1/2 teaspoon garlic powder
1/2 teaspoon ground coriander
1/4 teaspoon ground cumin
1/2 teaspoon salt
1/4 teaspoon black pepper
1 tablespoon canola oil

1. In a bowl, mash the white beans. Add the spinach and lemon juice and stir to combine. Add the walnuts, bread crumbs, flour, baking powder, onion powder, garlic powder, coriander, cumin, salt, and pepper, stirring until well mixed.

2. Heat the oil in a nonstick skillet over medium heat. Drop large spoonfuls of the mixture onto the hot skillet, in batches if needed. Flatten with a metal spatula and cook until browned on the bottom, about 5 minutes. Flip the fritters and cook until the other side is golden brown. Serve hot.

MAKES 4 SERVINGS

High-Water Hoppin' John

Southerners eat Hoppin' John and collards on New Year's Day for prosperity and good fortune in the coming year. "Come hell or high water" you can make an emergency variation of this "good luck" dish. Usually, fresh collard greens are cooked separately and served alongside. In this version, canned or rehydrated greens are stirred in for a tasty one-dish meal. Tabasco can be added at the table by those who enjoy it.

1. Bring 2 cups of salted water to a boil in a large saucepan. Add the rice, onion, olive oil, and thyme. Reduce heat to low, cover and cook until the rice is tender, about 10 minutes.

2. Stir in the black-eyed peas, greens, and salt and pepper to taste. Heat until hot.

3. Serve with Tabasco at the table.

MAKES 4 SERVINGS

1 cup quick-cooking rice
1 tablespoon dehydrated onion
2 teaspoons olive oil
1/2 teaspoon dried thyme
1 (15.5-ounce) can black-eyed peas, drained
1 (15-ounce) can collard greens, drained or 3/4 cup dehydrated spinach, rehydrated (page 34)
Salt and black pepper
Tabasco

7

Pasta and Grain Main Dishes

These main-dish recipes use pasta and grains in creative and resourceful ways. Not only do they require a minimum of preparation and cooking time, they also boast good nutrition and look and taste terrific. You're not eating mere Pantry Cuisine here. These dishes teeter perilously close to haute cuisine.

Think of it: Without power, you can make recipes such as Pasta with White Beans and Olivada or Rice Noodles with Spicy Peanut Sauce. All you need is a heat source that can bring water to a boil. These dishes taste so good, you may want to make them even when you have plenty of fresh vegetables and a working stove.

Pasta and Grain Main Dishes

Kitchen-Sink Capellini

Ramen Fagiole

Pasta Improv

Puttanesca in a Pinch

Pasta with Creamy Pumpkin Sauce and Walnuts

Pasta with White Beans and Olivada

Last Resort Lasagna

Red Beans and Rice

High Road Lo-Mein

Asian-Style Vegetable Pancakes with Dipping Sauce

Wild Mushroom Rice Pilaf

Layered Tortilla Skillet

Jazzed-Up Jasmine Rice

Pantry Bulgur Pilaf

Quick Quinoa Pilaf

Rice Noodles with Spicy Peanut Sauce

Suddenly Sushi

Couscous Unplugged

Using Your Noodle

When you're unplugged, you'll need a strategy for cooking pasta and noodles. This will depend on your water and cooking fuel situation. Capellini (angel hair) and other ultra-thin pastas cook in less than 5 minutes, so they're a good choice when you need to conserve precious cooking fuel. However, if water is in short supply, then boiling enough water to cook the pasta would be impractical. Naturally, if water and fuel are abundant, use any variety of pasta you prefer. For those times when cooking fuel is low and the water supply is limited, you can use ramen noodle bricks. Just add enough boiling water to cover the ramen until softened and they're ready to use in any of the pasta recipes with no additional cooking needed.

Another alternative is to use certain Asian noodles, such as cellophane noodles or rice vermicelli, which also require only soaking in boiling water to soften. It's important to note that some Asian noodles may require just as much cooking as pasta. Check the labels to be sure you find varieties that only need soaking.

Quick Cooking Grains

Since many grains can take up to 45 minutes to an hour to cook, they are impractical when you're cooking with limited cooking fuel. The good news is there are a number of grains that barely need cooking at all, making them ideal to use in these pantry cuisine recipes. Couscous is a prime example, taking just 5 minutes to cook. Be sure to stock up on the whole-grain variety for optimum nutrition. Other quick-cooking grains include bulgur, the steamed crushed wheat kernels used to make tabbouleh, and kasha, also known as buckwheat groats, popular in Eastern European countries. You can also buy quick-cooking brown rice which cooks up in 10 minutes.

Kitchen-Sink Capellini

With so many goodies in this flavorful dish, you can omit an ingredient or two and it will still taste great. If you have Kalamata or other imported olives on hand, use them instead of the regular sliced black olives. Note: If you can't spare the water to boil capellini, substitute ramen noodle bricks and simply reconstitute with enough boiling water to cover.

1/2 cup sun-dried tomatoes

1 pound capellini or angel hair pasta

3 teaspoons olive oil

3 garlic cloves, minced

2 (14.5-ounce) cans diced tomatoes, drained

1 (15.5-ounce) can chickpeas, drained

1 (6-ounce) jar marinated artichoke hearts, drained and chopped

1 (4-ounce) can sliced black olives, drained

1 tablespoon capers, drained (optional)

1 teaspoon dried basil (or 1 tablespoon fresh basil, if available)

Salt and black pepper

1/4 cup toasted pine nuts (optional)

1. Place the sun-dried tomatoes in a small heat-proof bowl. Add boiling water and let sit for 10 minutes to soften. Drain and cut into 1/4-inch strips. Set aside.

2. Cook the pasta in a pot of boiling salted water until tender, about 4 minutes. Drain the pasta in a colander. Drizzle with 1 teaspoon of the olive oil, toss to coat with the oil, and set aside.

3. In the same pot, heat 2 teaspoons of the oil over medium heat. Add the garlic and cook until fragrant, 30 seconds. Stir in both kinds of tomatoes, chickpeas, artichoke hearts, olives, capers (if using), basil, and salt and pepper to taste. Cook until hot, about 5 minutes. Add the reserved pasta and toss gently to combine and heat through. Serve hot sprinkled with the pine nuts, if using.

MAKES 4 SERVINGS

Ramen Fagiole

East meets West in this tasty use of ramen noodles in the popular Tuscan bean and pasta dish. If you have enough fuel and water, cook elbow macaroni instead of using ramen.

1. Break the noodle bricks into small pieces and transfer to a saucepan with enough boiling water to cover. Stir to break up the noodles as they soften.

2. Add the remaining ingredients. Cook, stirring, over medium heat for 7 to 9 minutes, or until the ingredients are well blended and the mixture is hot. Taste and adjust seasonings, adding a bit more water or seasonings, if needed. Serve hot.

MAKES 4 SERVINGS

3 ramen noodle bricks
1 (14.5-ounce) can diced tomatoes, undrained
1 (15-ounce) can pinto or cannelini beans, drained
1/2 teaspoon dried basil
1/2 teaspoon garlic powder
1/4 teaspoon onion powder
1/4 teaspoon dried oregano
1/4 teaspoon crushed red pepper
Salt and black pepper

Pasta Improv

Sure, a jarred pasta sauce is easier, but if you feel like improvising your own tomato sauce, here's an easy way to do it. This flavorful sauce is made with pantry ingredients; however, fresh ingredients, such as an onion, tomatoes, or fresh herbs may be used if you have them on hand. Be sure to use fresh garlic, if you can, since garlic bulbs store well at room temperature. If you don't have fresh, substitute a small amount of garlic powder.

1 pound pasta of choice
2 tablespoons olive oil
3 garlic cloves, minced
1 (28-ounce) can crushed tomatoes
1 tablespoon dehydrated minced onion
3 tablespoons dry red wine
1/2 teaspoon crushed red pepper
2 tablespoons dried basil
1 teaspoon dried parsley
Salt and black pepper

1. Cook the pasta according to package directions. Drain well, toss with 1 tablespoon of the olive oil, and set it aside while you make the sauce.

2. Heat the remaining oil in the same pot over medium heat. Add the garlic and cook until fragrant, 30 seconds. Stir in the tomatoes, onion, wine, red pepper flakes, basil, and parsley. Season to taste with salt and pepper and simmer until hot.

3. Stir in the cooked pasta until heated through, tossing gently to combine. Serve hot.

MAKES 4 SERVINGS

Puttanesca in a Pinch

Imported black and green olives are best in this sauce, but if all you have is the regular supermarket variety, they can be used in a pinch.

1. Cook the pasta according to package directions. Drain the pasta and place in a large bowl, tossing with a little olive oil to prevent sticking.

2. Heat the oil in the same pot over medium heat. Add the garlic and cook until fragrant, about 30 seconds. Stir in the tomatoes, black and green olives, capers, red pepper flakes, and parsley. Season with salt and pepper to taste. Reduce heat to low and simmer for 10 minutes to blend flavors, stirring occasionally.

3. Add the reserved pasta and toss gently to combine and heat through.

MAKES 4 SERVINGS

1 pound pasta of choice
1 tablespoon olive oil
3 large garlic cloves, minced
1 (28-ounce) can crushed tomatoes
1/2 cup pitted and sliced black kalamata olives or
1 (4-ounce) can sliced black olives, drained
1/4 cup pitted and sliced green olives
2 tablespoons capers, drained and chopped
1/2 teaspoon crushed red pepper
1 teaspoon dried parsley
Salt and freshly ground black pepper

Pasta with Creamy Pumpkin Sauce and Walnuts

Pasta tossed with a creamy sage-infused sauce sprinkled with walnuts is good enough to make you forget this is Pantry Cuisine. If water is at a premium, scratch the angel hair pasta in favor of pouring a small amount of boiling water over a few ramen noodle bricks (drain and proceed with recipe).

1 (15-ounce) can solid-pack pumpkin
1 cup water
1 teaspoon vegetable broth base
1 teaspoon ground sage
1 teaspoon garlic powder
1/2 teaspoon onion powder
12 ounces angel hair pasta or cappelini
1/2 cup chopped toasted walnuts

1. In a saucepan, combine the pumpkin, water, broth base, sage, garlic powder, and onion powder. Cook over medium heat until smooth and hot. Season with salt and pepper to taste. If the sauce is too thick, add a little water. Set aside.

2. Cook the pasta in a pot of boiling salted water until tender, 3 to 4 minutes. Drain and return to the pot. Add the reserved sauce and toss to combine. Serve sprinkled with the walnuts.

MAKES 4 SERVINGS

Pasta with White Beans and Olivada

If you're lucky enough to have imported olives on hand, make olivada, a rich Mediterranean olive paste that goes great with pasta. You can use a mortar and pestle to mash them, or finely chop the olives and garlic with a knife. Be advised: this recipe is for card-carrying olive lovers.

1. Finely chop the olives and garlic. Transfer to a mortar and pestle and add the lemon juice, basil, and salt and pepper to taste. Work the mixture until blended. Slowly add the olive oil and process to a paste. Set aside.

2. Place the ramen bricks in a heatproof bowl. Add enough boiling water to cover. Set aside for 5 minutes to soften. Remove 3 tablespoons of the hot pasta water and blend it into the olivada.

3. Place the beans in a colander and drain the noodles into the colander. This will heat and rinse the beans at the same time. Place the drained pasta and beans in a large serving bowl. Add the reserved olivada and toss gently to combine. Serve hot.

MAKES 4 SERVINGS

8 ounces kalamata or other imported black olives, pitted
1 large garlic clove
2 teaspoons lemon juice
1/2 teaspoon dried basil
Salt and black pepper
2 tablespoons olive oil
4 ramen noodle bricks
1 (15.5-ounce) can Great Northern or other white beans, drained

Last Resort Lasagna

Without the use of an oven, this is as close as you can get to real lasagna, though the results are surprisingly good. You can jazz this dish up by adding reconstituted TVP granules to the tomato sauce.

9 lasagna noodles
1 (15.5-ounce) can white beans, drained
1 (12-ounce) box firm silken tofu, drained
1/3 cup nutritional yeast
1 teaspoon dried parsley
1/2 teaspoon dried basil
1/4 teaspoon dried oregano
1/2 teaspoon onion powder
1/2 teaspoon garlic powder
Salt and black pepper
1 (28-ounce) jar marinara sauce

1. Arrange the lasagna noodles in a shallow baking pan and cover with boiling water. Set aside for 5 minutes to soften.

2. In a bowl, combine the beans, tofu, 1/4 cup of nutritional yeast, parsley, basil, oregano, onion powder, garlic powder, and salt and pepper to taste. Mash well until smooth and well combined. Taste to adjust seasoning.

3. In a large skillet, over medium-low heat, spread 3/4 cup of the sauce and place 3 of the softened noodles on top, overlapping slightly. Spread half of the tofu and bean mixture on top of the noodles, and top with 3 more noodles. Spread a small amount of sauce on top and spread the remaining filling mixture over it. Top with the remaining 3 noodles and spread the remaining sauce over the noodles. Sprinkle the remaining nutritional yeast on top of the sauce.

4. Cover the skillet tightly with a lid and cook until the noodles are tender and the filling is hot,

about 15 minutes. Remove from heat and let
stand for 5 minutes before serving.

MAKES 4 SERVINGS

Red Beans and Rice

Brown rice is more nutritious than white and is available in a "quick-cooking" version that takes only 10 minutes.

1. Heat the oil in a saucepan over medium heat.
   Add the garlic and cook until fragrant, 30 seconds. Stir in the rice to coat with oil. Add the
   onion, chiles, salt, thyme, and cumin, stirring
   to combine.

2. Stir in the water, cover, and cook until the rice
   is tender, 8 to 10 minutes. Stir in the beans and
   cook until hot, about 5 minutes longer. Taste to
   adjust seasonings.

MAKES 4 SERVINGS

1 tablespoon olive oil
3 garlic cloves, minced
2 cups quick-cooking brown rice
1 tablespoon dehydrated minced
    onion
1 (4-ounce) can chopped mild
    green chiles, drained
1/2 teaspoon salt
1/2 teaspoon dried thyme
1/2 teaspoon ground cumin
2 1/4 cups water
1 (15.5-ounce) can dark red kid-
    ney beans, drained

High-Road Lo-Mein

Without fresh veggies, you can take the high road and make lo-mein with ingredients from your pantry. If you have fresh or frozen veggies on hand, add some frozen green peas or use a shredded fresh carrot in place of canned or dehydrated. Spice it up with a drizzle of Chinese hot oil.

3 to 4 ramen noodle bricks
2 teaspoons toasted sesame oil
1/4 cup soy sauce
3 tablespoons dry sherry
Pinch sugar
2 teaspoons canola oil
2 shallots, halved lengthwise and
    thinly sliced
2 teaspoons grated fresh ginger
    (optional)
1 cup reconstituted Soy Curls
    (optional)
1 (8-ounce) can sliced carrots,
    drained or 1/4 cup dehydrated
    carrots, rehydrated (page 34)
1 (8-ounce) can water chestnuts,
    drained
1 (8-ounce) can bamboo shoots,
    drained

1. Break the ramen noodle bricks in half and place in a heatproof bowl with enough boiling water to cover. When softened, drain the water and add 1 teaspoon of the sesame oil to the noodles, tossing to coat. Set aside.

2. In a small bowl, combine the soy sauce, sherry, sugar, and remaining 1 teaspoon of sesame oil. Set aside.

3. Heat the canola oil in a saucepan over medium heat. Add the shallots, ginger (if using), Soy Curls (if using), and carrot and stir-fry for 1 minute. Add the noodles, water chestnuts, bamboo shoots, and the reserved sauce and stir-fry to combine and heat through until hot, about 3 minutes.

MAKES 4 SERVINGS

Asian-Style Vegetable Pancakes
with Dipping Sauce

These pancakes are easy to make and fun to eat. Best of all, they even make canned vegetables taste good.

1. *Dipping Sauce:* In a small bowl, combine all the sauce ingredients and mix well. Set aside.

2. *Pancakes:* In a medium bowl, combine the flours, salt, garlic powder, and sesame seeds. Stir in the water and mix until blended. Add the vegetables and stir to combine.

3. Heat 1 tablespoon canola oil in a large non-stick skillet over medium heat. Ladle about one fourth of the batter into the hot skillet, tilting the pan to form a thin pancake. Cook until firm and nicely browned, about 6 minutes. Flip the pancake to cook the other side for 3 minutes.

4. Transfer the pancake to a plate and cover with foil to keep warm while you cook the remaining pancakes, adding more oil to the pan as needed. Serve hot with the dipping sauce on the side.

MAKES 4 SERVINGS

Dipping Sauce:
1/4 cup soy sauce
3 tablespoons rice vinegar
2 tablespoons sake or mirin
2 tablespoons water
1 teaspoon toasted sesame oil
1 teaspoon sugar
1/2 teaspoon hot chili oil or
    crushed red pepper

Pancakes:
1/2 cup all-purpose flour
2 tablespoons tapioca flour or
    potato starch
1/2 teaspoon salt
1/4 teaspoon garlic powder
1 teaspoon sesame seeds
3/4 cup water
1 (15-ounce) can chow mein
    vegetables, drained and finely
    chopped
Canola oil, for frying

Wild Mushroom Rice Pilaf

When the power is out, I think it's remarkable to be able to enjoy a wild mushroom pilaf instead of peanut butter crackers. 'Nuf said.

1/4 cup dried mushrooms
1 cup quick-cooking rice
1 tablespoon olive oil
3 tablespoons pine nuts
1 (14-ounce) can asparagus tips, drained or 1/2 cup dehydrated asparagus, rehydrated (see page 34)
1/2 teaspoon garlic powder
1 tablespoon lemon juice
Salt and black pepper

1. Place the mushrooms in a heatproof bowl with enough boiling water to cover. Set aside for 10 minutes to soften. Cook the rice in a saucepan until tender. Set aside.

2. Heat the oil in a skillet over medium heat. Add the pine nuts and cook until lightly toasted. Add the asparagus, garlic powder, lemon juice, and reserved rice. Drain the mushrooms and add them to the rice mixture. Stir to combine and heat until hot. Season with salt and pepper to taste. Serve hot.

MAKES 4 SERVINGS

Layered Tortilla Skillet

Salsa, chiles, pinto beans, and tortillas team up for a zesty "baked" casserole. If you have any vegan cheddar cheese, sprinkle it on top. Otherwise, a light dusting of nutritional yeast or vegan Parmesan works to good effect.

1. In a bowl, combine the pinto beans, chiles, chili powder, and oregano. Stir in half the salsa and mix well. Season with salt and pepper to taste. Mash the pinto mixture well to break up ingredients. Set aside.

2. Cover the bottom of a deep skillet with half of the remaining salsa. Top with half of the tortillas, overlapping as necessary. Top the tortillas with the reserved bean mixture. Then top with the remaining tortillas. Spread the remaining salsa mixture over all.

3. Cover with a tight fitting lid and cook over low heat for 15 minutes to heat through. Sprinkle with nutritional yeast, if using.

MAKES 4 SERVINGS

2 (15.5-ounce) cans pinto beans, drained
1 (4-ounce) can chopped green chiles, drained (hot or mild)
1 teaspoon chili powder, or more to taste
1/4 teaspoon dried oregano
1 (16-ounce) jar salsa (hot or mild)
Salt and black pepper
8 (7-inch) flour tortillas
Nutritional yeast (optional)

Jazzed-Up Jasmine Rice

You'll need to cook the rice first and then let it cool before making this recipe. If jasmine rice is unavailable, use quick-cooking brown rice instead. If canned stir-fry vegetables are unavailable, substitute canned or rehydrated mixed vegetables or fine slivers of any fresh veggies you may have on hand, such as carrots or onion.

1 tablespoon canola oil
2 garlic cloves, minced
2 teaspoons grated fresh ginger (optional)
1 (15-ounce) can mixed vegetables, drained or 3/4 cup dehydrated vegetable flakes, rehydrated (page 34)
3 1/2 cups cooked jasmine rice
2 tablespoons soy sauce
1/2 teaspoon onion powder
1/2 teaspoon light brown sugar
1/2 cup chopped roasted cashews

1. Heat the oil in a large skillet or wok over medium high heat. Add the garlic and ginger (if using) and cook until fragrant, 30 seconds.

2. Add the vegetables and rice and stir fry until combined. Add the soy sauce, onion powder, and sugar and stir-fry until the ingredients are blended and hot, about 5 minutes.

3. Sprinkle with chopped cashews and serve hot.

MAKES 4 SERVINGS

Pantry Bulgur Pilaf

Also called cracked wheat, bulgur is a quick-cooking grain with a hearty nut-like flavor that is used to make the popular Middle Eastern salad, tabbouleh. This yummy pilaf with sweet/tart cranberries and crunchy almonds will help you make the best of it.

1. Bring the broth to a boil in a large saucepan. Add the bulgur and onion and stir to combine.

2. Reduce the heat to low and season with salt and pepper to taste. Cover and simmer until the bulgur is tender and the liquid is absorbed, about 8 minutes.

3. Remove the pan from the heat and stir in the cranberries, almonds, and parsley or mint. Cover and let stand for 10 minutes.

MAKES 4 SERVINGS

2 cups vegetable broth (see page 119)
1 cup medium bulgur
1 tablespoon dehydrated minced onion
Salt and freshly ground black pepper
1/2 cup dried cranberries
1/2 cup toasted slivered almonds
1 teaspoon dried parsley or mint (or 1 tablespoon fresh, if you've got it)

Quick Quinoa Pilaf

Extremely high in protein and quick-cooking, quinoa is an ideal grain for Pantry Cuisine. It adapts deliciously to various seasonings and is especially delicious when prepared pilaf-style. Quinoa is available in natural food stores. Did you know quinoa was enjoyed by the Incas?

1 1/2 cups quinoa
3 cups hot vegetable broth (see page 119) or water
1 tablespoon dehydrated minced onion
Salt and freshly ground black pepper
1 (8-ounce) can sliced carrots, drained or 1/3 cup dehydrated carrots, rehydrated (page 34)
1 (8-ounce) can green peas, drained or 1/3 cup dehydrated green peas, rehydrated (page 34)
1/4 cup toasted pine nuts
1 tablespoon dried chives

1. Rinse the quinoa well to remove the bitter white coating. Drain it thoroughly and set aside.

2. Bring the broth or water to a boil. Add the quinoa and onion. Reduce the heat to low and season to taste with salt and pepper. Cover and cook until the water is absorbed, about 12 minutes.

3. Remove from the heat. Stir in the carrots, peas, pine nuts, and chives. Serve hot.

MAKES 4 SERVINGS

Rice Noodles with Spicy Peanut Sauce

If you don't have thin rice noodles that require soaking rather than cooking in boiling water, you can use ramen noodles instead. Our supermarket carries canned "stir-fry" vegetables, a combination of water chestnuts, bamboo shoots, bean sprouts, and baby corn. If unavailable, substitute fresh or rehydrated vegetables of choice.

1. Soak the noodles in boiling water until soft, about 15 minutes. While the noodles are softening, prepare the sauce.

2. In a bowl, whisk together the peanut butter, soy sauce, vinegar, sugar, red pepper flakes, and 1/2 cup of the water. Blend until smooth.

3. Transfer the peanut sauce to a large pot and stir in as much of the remaining water as needed to give it a desirable consistency. Heat the sauce over low heat, stirring until it is hot. Stir in the vegetables and heat through until hot. Keep warm.

4. Drain the softened noodles and add to the pot. Toss gently to combine with the peanut sauce. Serve sprinkled with the peanuts.

MAKES 4 SERVINGS

8 ounces thin rice noodles

1/2 cup peanut butter

3 tablespoons soy sauce

1 tablespoon rice vinegar

1 teaspoon brown sugar

1/2 teaspoon red pepper flakes, or to taste

1 cup water

1 (15-ounce) can stir-fry vegetables, drained

2 tablespoons chopped roasted peanuts

Suddenly Sushi

Sushi-making ingredients are available at well-stocked supermarkets, natural food stores, and Asian markets. If you don't have a *sudare* (bamboo sushi mat), you can roll your makis in a clean cloth napkin or sheet of plastic wrap.

2 cups quick-cooking rice
2 tablespoons rice vinegar
1 tablespoon sugar
1/2 teaspoon salt
6 roasted nori sheets
2 tablespoons toasted sesame
    seeds
Filling options (choose two):
    canned asparagus spears,
    drained and patted dry;
    hearts of palm, cut into strips;
    kanpyo (dried gourd strip),
    reconstituted; roasted red
    pepper strips; jarred fried
    wheat gluten, cut into strips
1 tablespoon wasabi powder
1 tablespoon warm water
2 tablespoons pickled ginger for
    garnish
Tamari soy sauce

1. Cook the rice in boiling water according to package directions. Transfer the rice to a shallow bowl and mix in the vinegar, sugar, and salt. Spread the rice evenly using a rice paddle or large wooden spoon. Set aside to cool.

2. Place a sheet of nori on a sudare or a cloth napkin. Spread 1/2 cup of the rice evenly over the nori sheet to the edge on the sides and to within 1 inch on the top and bottom edges. Sprinkle the rice evenly with the sesame seeds. Along the edge nearest to you, place a row of filling ingredients on top of the rice.

3. Beginning at the end nearest you, roll up the sudare, pressing firmly against the nori to roll around the ingredients, using your fingers to keep the end of the sudare from rolling into the sushi. Continue rolling slowly up to the top edge. Wet the exposed edge of the nori with a bit of water to seal the roll. Gently squeeze the sudare around the sushi roll and remove the mat.

4. Use a sharp knife to cut the sushi roll into 6 pieces, wiping the blade between cuts. Stand the pieces on end and place on a large platter. Make additional rolls with the remaining ingredients.

5. In a small bowl, combine the wasabi powder with the warm water to form a paste. Place a small mound of the wasabi paste onto the sushi platter. Arrange a pile of pickled ginger on the platter, as well. Pour tamari into small dipping bowls to serve alongside.

NOTE: To save fuel, this sushi is made with quick-cooking "minute-type" rice instead of the long-cooking traditional sushi rice, which is glutinous and holds together better. Since quick-cooking rice is a bit looser, you'll need to press the rice into the nori a bit more so it holds together.

MAKES 6 ROLLS OR 36 PIECES

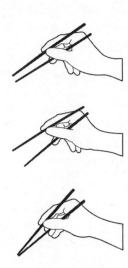

Couscous Unplugged

What do you do when you're famished and don't feel like cooking? Try this almost-instant couscous pilaf. It's tasty, filling, and ready in 10 minutes. If you have a fresh carrot, you can substitute it for the canned or dehydrated vegetables. Simply shred the carrot on a box grater and add it when you add the couscous. The bits of carrot will soften up nicely.

2 cups water or vegetable broth (see page 119)
1 cup couscous
1 tablespoon dehydrated minced onion
1 teaspoon ground coriander
1/2 teaspoon ground cumin
1/4 teaspoon ground cayenne
1 (15.5-ounce) can chickpeas, drained
1 (15-ounce) can mixed vegetables, drained or 3/4 cup dehydrated vegetable flakes, rehydrated (page 34)
1/2 cup chopped pecans or slivered almonds
1/4 cup golden or regular raisins
Salt and black pepper

1. Bring the water to a boil in a saucepan. Stir in the couscous, onion, coriander, cumin, and cayenne. Cover, turn off the heat and let sit for 10 minutes.

2. Stir in the chickpeas, vegetables, pecans, and raisins. Season to taste with salt and pepper and serve.

MAKES 4 SERVINGS

8

Salad Days

This collection of delicious salads will add color, texture, and extra flavor to the nonperishable vegetables waiting for you in your Pantry Cuisine. Many of these salads make use of quick-cooking grains and noodles, along with beans and nuts, to make them substantial enough to serve as a main dish for lunch or a light supper. It's important to note that many of these salads would be even better if served on a bed of fresh salad greens. If you have some lettuce in the fridge or garden, these salads are a great way to use them up.

Salads Days

Five-Minute Couscous Salad

Amazing Technicolor Chickpea Salad

"Make Mine Moroccan" Couscous Salad

Towering Tabbouleh Salad

Pantry Pasta Salad

Composed Marinated Vegetable Salad

Corn, Tomatillo, and Red Pepper Salad

Nutty Ramen Salad

Southwest Salmagundi

Three's-a-Crowd Bean Salad

Niçoise Salad

Asian Noodle Salad with Peanut Dressing

Hearts of Palm Salad

Five-Minute Couscous Salad

Couscous is ideal for Pantry Cuisine. Unlike some other grains which can take up to 45 minutes to cook, couscous takes just five minutes. Be sure to stock up on the whole-grain variety for optimum nutrition. As is, the recipe is a main-dish salad for four, but can be easily halved for two.

1. In a saucepan, combine the water and bouillon cube, and bring to a boil. Stir in the couscous, cover the saucepan, and remove it from the heat. Let the mixture stand for 5 minutes.

2. Stir in the almonds, parsley, olive oil, vinegar, chives, and salt and pepper to taste. Mix well.

3. Mound in the center of a platter surrounded by the three-bean salad.

MAKES 4 SERVINGS

2 1/2 cups water
1 vegetable bouillon cube or 1 teaspoon vegetable soup base
2 cups whole-grain couscous
1/2 cup slivered almonds, lightly toasted
2 teaspoons dried parsley flakes (or 2 tablespoons fresh parsley, if available)
2 tablespoons olive oil
1 tablespoon white wine vinegar
2 teaspoons dried minced chives
Salt and black pepper
2 (16-ounce) jars three-bean salad, drained

Amazing Technicolor Chickpea Salad

When you need something to make you smile, try this salad. A combination of chickpeas, beets, and pineapple, it delivers good nutrition while lighting up your taste buds. The vibrant pink color may make you reach for you sunglasses.

1 (8-ounce) can sliced beets,
  drained
1 (15.5-ounce) can chickpeas,
  drained
1 (8-ounce) can chunk pineapple,
  drained with juice reserved
1 tablespoon olive oil
1 teaspoon lemon juice
1/4 teaspoon sugar
Salt and black pepper

1. Cut the beets into 1/4-inch dice and transfer to a medium bowl. Add the chickpeas and pineapple chunks.

2. Drizzle on about 1/3 cup of the reserved pineapple juice, the oil, lemon juice, and sugar. Season with salt and pepper, and mix well.

MAKES 4 SERVINGS

"Make Mine Moroccan" Couscous Salad

Fragrant spices make this salad the one to choose when you want something that will shake up the routine. Brimming with a variety of flavors and textures, it takes only a few minutes to prepare.

1. Heat 1/2 tablespoon of the oil in a medium saucepan over low heat. Add the turmeric, cinnamon, ginger, cumin, cayenne, and couscous and stir until fragrant, about 1 minute. Do not burn. Stir in the water and juice and bring to a boil. Reduce the heat to very low, cover and cook 5 minutes. Remove from the heat and let stand about 5 minutes longer.

2. Transfer the couscous to a large bowl, using a fork to fluff it up. Stir in the remaining 1/2 tablespoon of oil, the sugar, and salt to taste.

3. Add the chickpeas, carrots, dried fruit, and raisins. Toss gently to combine. Garnish with peanuts.

MAKES 4 SERVINGS

1 tablespoon olive oil
1/4 teaspoon ground turmeric
1/4 teaspoon ground cinnamon
1/4 teaspoon ground ginger
1/4 teaspoon ground cumin
1/4 teaspoon cayenne
1 1/2 cups couscous
1 1/4 cups water
1 cup apple juice
1 teaspoon light brown sugar
Salt
1 (15.5-ounce) can chickpeas, drained
1 (8-ounce) can sliced carrots, drained or 1/4 cup dehydrated carrots, rehydrated (page 34)
1/4 cup chopped dried fruit
1/4 cup golden raisins
2 tablespoons chopped unsalted peanuts

Towering Tabbouleh Salad

Just for a bit of aesthetic fun, the tabbouleh salad is packed into ring molds to create "tower" shapes. Use ring molds, if you have them, or cut the bottom off an empty, squat 4-ounce can, such as those containing green chiles. Alternately, the salad may simply be spooned onto plates or bowls.

2 cups water
1 cup medium-grind bulgur
1 tablespoon dehydrated onion
1 (14.5-ounce) can diced tomatoes, drained and chopped
1 (15.5-ounce) can chickpeas, drained
1 teaspoon dried parsley or 1 tablespoon fresh, if available
1/2 teaspoon dried mint, or 1 teaspoon fresh, if available
3 tablespoons olive oil
2 tablespoons lemon juice
Salt and black pepper

1. Bring the water to a boil in a saucepan and add the bulgur and onion. Reduce heat to low, cover, and simmer for 15 minutes, or until water is absorbed. Drain any remaining water and blot the bulgur to remove excess moisture.

2. Place the bulgur in a bowl and allow to cool. Add the tomatoes, chickpeas, parsley, and mint.

3. In a small bowl combine the olive oil, lemon juice, and salt and pepper to taste. Pour the dressing over the salad and toss well to combine.

4. To serve, place a ring mold on a salad plate and pack the salad mixture inside. Remove the mold and repeat, making two "towers" per serving.

MAKES 4 SERVINGS

Pantry Pasta Salad

The great thing about this recipe is that the portion size is easy to adjust. This version makes four average servings, or enough for two or three hungry eaters. To increase the volume, cook an entire pound of pasta and add additional pantry goodies, such as olives, roasted red peppers, or pine nuts.

1. If using capellini, break the strands into thirds and cook the pasta in a pot of boiling salted water, stirring occasionally, until it is al dente, about 3 minutes. If using ramen, break the noodle bricks into quarters and place in a bowl. Cover with boiling water and set aside to soften.

2. Drain the chickpeas into a colander and, when the pasta is cooked, drain it into the same colander, allowing the pasta water to rinse the chickpeas. Transfer the pasta and chickpeas to a large bowl, toss with 1 teaspoon of the olive oil and set aside.

3. In a small bowl, combine the lemon juice, tarragon, and salt and pepper to taste. Whisk in the remaining olive oil until blended and pour dressing over pasta. Add the artichokes and sun-dried tomatoes, and toss to combine.

MAKES 4 SERVINGS

12 ounces capellini or 3 ramen noodle bricks
1 (15.5-ounce) can chickpeas, drained
3 tablespoons plus 1 teaspoon olive oil
2 tablespoons lemon juice
1 teaspoon dried tarragon
Salt and black pepper
1 (6-ounce) can marinated artichoke hearts, drained
3 to 4 sun-dried tomatoes, reconstituted and cut into thin strips

Composed Marinated Vegetable Salad

Despite its humble origins in your pantry hoard, this salad draws its inspiration both from a French *salade composé* and an Italian antipasto, wherein you artfully arrange the salad components on a platter.

3 tablespoons olive oil

1 1/2 tablespoons balsamic vinegar

1/2 teaspoon minced garlic

1/2 teaspoon dried basil

Salt and black pepper

1 (8-ounce) can cut green beans, drained or 1/4 cup dehydrated green beans, rehydrated (page 34)

1 (4-ounce) jar roasted red bell peppers, drained and cut into strips

1 (15-ounce) can sliced potatoes, drained

1 (6-ounce) jar marinated artichoke hearts, drained

1 (4-ounce) can sliced black olives, drained

2 tablespoons toasted pine nuts (optional)

1. In a small bowl combine the olive oil, balsamic vinegar, garlic, basil, salt, and pepper. Whisk to combine. Set aside.

2. Arrange the green beans, bell peppers, potatoes, and artichoke hearts on a large platter. Drizzle the reserved dressing evenly over all. Nestle the olives decoratively among the vegetables. Sprinkle with pine nuts, if using, and serve.

MAKES 4 SERVINGS

Corn, Tomatillo, and Red Pepper Salad

To turn this into a main dish salad, just add a can of pinto beans. It will add extra protein while maintaining the Southwestern theme.

1. In a large bowl, combine the corn, tomatillos, and bell pepper.

2. In a small bowl, combine the shallot, lime juice, cumin, salt, and cayenne. Whisk in the oil to emulsify.

3. Pour the dressing over the salad and toss lightly to coat. Taste to adjust seasonings.

MAKES 4 SERVINGS

1 (15-ounce) can corn kernels, drained or 3/4 cup dehydrated corn kernels, rehydrated (pae 34)
1 (14-ounce) can tomatillos, drained and chopped
1 (8-ounce) can roasted red bell peppers, drained and chopped
1 shallot, minced
1 1/2 tablespoons lime juice or lemon juice
1/4 teaspoon ground cumin
1/2 teaspoon salt
1/8 teaspoon cayenne
3 tablespoons olive oil

NATURAL PRESERVATIVES

Foods containing acids, such as lemon juice and vinegar, or pickled foods, such as capers and pickles, will last longer unrefrigerated, if you keep them covered in the preserving liquid and the lid on tight. Store them in the coolest spot possible. (See pages 51 and 171 for food safety tips.)

Nutty Ramen Salad

If you're looking for different way to prepare ramen, how about turning it into a salad? It tastes delicious and, with the addition of the slivered almonds, has a nutty flavor. As always, toss out the seasoning packets that come with the ramen noodles.

2 ramen noodle bricks, broken into 1-inch pieces
1 tablespoon dehydrated onion
1 (14-ounce) can bean sprouts, drained
1 tablespoon canola oil
1/2 cup slivered almonds
1/4 cup sunflower seeds
3 tablespoons sesame seeds
2 tablespoons rice wine vinegar
1 tablespoon toasted sesame oil
1 teaspoon sugar
1/4 teaspoon celery salt
1/4 teaspoon garlic powder
1/4 teaspoon cayenne (optional)
1 tablespoon soy sauce

1. Place the noodles in a small saucepan with enough boiling water to cover. Reduce heat to low, add the dehydrated onion, and cook for 1 minute. Drain the bean sprouts in a colander and, when the noodles are cooked, drain them in the same colander to rinse the bean sprouts. Transfer the noodles and bean sprouts to a bowl and set aside.

2. Heat the canola oil in a skillet over medium heat. Add the almonds and cook, stirring, until golden brown, about 5 minutes. Add the sunflower seeds and continue to cook until sesame seeds turn golden brown, 1 to 2 minutes longer. Add to the noodle mixture and toss to combine.

3. Add the vinegar, sesame oil, sugar, celery salt, garlic powder, cayenne (if using), and soy sauce, tossing well to coat. Cover and let stand for 15 minutes before serving.

MAKES 4 SERVINGS

Southwest Salmagundi

Spicy food lovers may want to use hot salsa rather than mild. The asbestos-tongued may go a step further and substitute canned sliced jalapeños for the mild green chiles.

1. In a large bowl, combine the pinto beans, chiles, parsley, olive oil, lime juice, chili powder, cumin, garlic powder, and salt to taste. Stir gently to combine.

2. Spread the heated refried beans in the center of a large plate, mound the pinto bean salad on top and arrange a border of salsa around the outside perimeter of the salad. Surround with tortilla chips.

MAKES 4 SERVINGS

1 (15.5-ounce) can pinto beans, drained
1 (4-ounce) can chopped mild green chiles, drained
1 teaspoon dried parsley
2 tablespoons olive oil
1 tablespoon lime juice or lemon juice
1/2 teaspoon chili powder
1/4 teaspoon ground cumin
1/4 teaspoon garlic powder
Salt
1 (16-ounce) can vegan refried beans, heated
1 (8-ounce) jar mild or hot salsa
Tortilla chips, as desired

Three's-a-Crowd Bean Salad

For a change of pace, try creating your own version of three-bean salad. This version leaves out the green or waxed beans and feature kidney beans and chickpeas instead. You can also go all out and add canned or reconstituted dehydrated of cut green beans.

1 (15.5-ounce) can chickpeas, drained
1 (15.5-ounce) can kidney beans, drained
1 (2-ounce) jar chopped pimientos, drained
1 tablespoon dehydrated minced onion
2 tablespoons white wine vinegar
1 teaspoon sugar
1/2 teaspoon salt
1/8 teaspoon cayenne
3 tablespoons olive oil

1. In a large bowl, combine the chickpeas, kidney beans, pimientos, and onion and set aside.

2. In a small bowl, combine the vinegar, sugar, salt, and cayenne. Whisk in the oil to emulsify.

3. Pour the dressing over the salad and toss lightly to coat. Taste to adjust seasonings.

MAKES 4 SERVINGS

Niçoise Salad

A Niçoise salad makes a flavorful and colorful main-dish salad—even if you're using pantry ingredients. If you can score some fresh lettuce on which to bed this salad, go for it. If you have fresh green beans, tomatoes, and potatoes, too, well then, you should just go and make yourself a fresh salad, shouldn't you?

1. In a large bowl, combine the green beans, potatoes, tomatoes, white beans, and olives.

2. In a small bowl, whisk together the remaining ingredients and add to the ingredients in the large bowl. Toss gently to combine. Taste to adjust seasonings.

MAKES 4 SERVINGS

1 (15-ounce) can cut green beans, drained or 3/4 cup dehydrated green beans, rehydrated (page 34)

1 (15-ounce) can whole white potatoes, drained and diced

1 (14.5-ounce) can diced tomatoes, drained

1 (15.5-ounce) can white beans, drained

1 (4-ounce) can sliced black olives, drained

3 tablespoons olive oil

1 1/2 tablespoon white balsamic vinegar

1/2 teaspoon dry mustard

1 teaspoon dried basil

1/4 teaspoon salt

Black pepper

Asian Noodle Salad with Peanut Dressing

This tangle of noodles with a peanut dressing upgrade tastes great. If you like more heat, add another 1/4 teaspoon of red pepper flakes. If you don't like heat, leave it out.

1/2 cup peanut butter
3 tablespoons soy sauce
2 tablespoons rice wine vinegar
1/2 teaspoon light brown sugar
1/4 teaspoon red pepper flakes, or to taste
1/8 teaspoon garlic powder
1/2 cup water
12 ounces thin rice vermicelli or ramen noodles
2 teaspoons toasted sesame oil
1 (8-ounce) can sliced carrots, drained or 1/4 cup dehydrated carrots, rehydrated (page 34)
1 (8-ounce) can water chestnuts, drained
1 (8-ounce) can straw mushrooms, drained
1/4 cup dry roasted peanuts

1. In a bowl, combine the peanut butter, soy sauce, vinegar, red pepper flakes, and garlic powder, stirring to blend well. Add the water, stirring until smooth. Set aside.

2. Soak the noodles in enough boiling water to cover until softened. Drain and transfer to a large bowl. Toss with sesame oil to coat.

3. Add the carrots, water chestnuts, mushrooms, and peanuts to the bowl with the noodles. Add the reserved peanut sauce, tossing gently to combine.

MAKES 4 SERVINGS

Hearts of Palm Salad

Achieving the colors, textures, and flavors of this knock-out salad is easy. Just be sure not to skimp on the seasonings.

1. In a large bowl, combine the hearts of palm, limas, red peppers, and olives. Add the oil, lemon juice, chives, mustard, basil, marjoram, salt, and pepper. Toss gently to combine.

2. Cover and set aside at room temperature for about 10 minutes before serving to allow flavors to blend. Taste and adjust the seasonings before serving.

MAKES 4 SERVINGS

1 (14-ounce) can hearts of palm, cut into 1/4-inch rounds

1 (15-ounce) can lima beans, drained or 3/4 cup dehydrated limas or peas, rehydrated (page 34)

1 (8-ounce) jar roasted red pepper, drained and cut into strips

1/4 cup kalamata olives, pitted and sliced

3 tablespoons olive oil

2 tablespoons lemon juice

1 teaspoon dried minced chives

1/2 teaspoon dry mustard

1/2 teaspoon dried basil

1/4 teaspoon dried marjoram

1/4 teaspoon salt

1/8 teaspoon black pepper

9

Soothing Soups

A bowl of comforting soup can be an ideal mealtime solution not only when the power is out, but for those times when you don't feel like cooking. Many soups normally must simmer for an hour, but if you're unplugged, you won't have enough fuel for that. The solution is these simple soups, which use quick-cooking ingredients that produce rich-tasting results after only a few minutes of cooking time. From a hearty Black Bean Soup with a Whisper of Sherry to a remarkable Instant Vichyssoise, this chapter is filled with quick and easy soups that satisfy.

Soothing Soups

Flaky Potato-Peanut Soup

White Beans and Greens Soup

Emergency Gazpacho

Black Bean Soup with a Whisper of Sherry

Shiitake Happens Mushroom Soup

Instant Vichyssoise

Hot and Sour Soup

Pretty Good Gumbo

Use-It-Up Minestrone Soup

Curry-Spiced Pumpkin Bisque

Comforting Corn Chowder

Artichoke, Shiitake, and White Bean Soup

How to Make Vegetable Broth

You may be wondering how to make vegetable broth, since everyone knows a good stock needs at least an hour to cook. Unless you have a working gas stove, you may not have the kind of fuel needed to simmer a pot of stock. Here are some options from your Pantry Stash:

- broth in aseptic containers
- canned broth
- bouillon cubes
- powdered soup base

When a recipe calls for "2 cups vegetable broth," you can use any of the above items to make it. As with any packaged food, check the ingredients first to make sure it's vegan and also for any additives. Some of these are high in sodium and contain corn syrup, MSG, and other additives. When using commercial broths, taste them for strength (some are quite strong in flavor). You can easily cut canned broth with water for a milder result. For example, if a recipe calls for 4 cups of broth, use 1 can (2 cups) of broth plus 2 cups of water. This is also more economical, since some of these broths can be pricey.

The most economical choice (which also economizes on space) is bouillon cubes or powdered soup bases. We favor the Vogue Cuisine brand powdered soup base. They are made with mostly organic ingredients, have a good flavor, no MSG or other additives, and boast reduced sodium. One 12-ounce plastic jar is enough to make 75 cups of broth. Vogue products (and other brands) are available in natural food stores.

Flaky Potato-Peanut Soup

The secret ingredient in this rich, creamy peanut soup is the instant potato flakes. And it's not as flaky as you might think, because of how well the flavors work together. The best part about this soup is that the flavor can be altered to suit your mood. Feel like Thai? Add a smidge of lime juice, soy sauce, and chili paste. For an Indian flair, stir in some curry powder. Or to simply jazz it up, add fresh or dried herb of choice.

4 cups vegetable broth (see page 119)
1 cup instant potato flakes
1/2 cup creamy peanut butter
1/4 teaspoon celery salt
1/8 teaspoon onion powder
Black pepper
1/4 cup chopped dry-roasted peanuts

1. Bring the broth to a boil in a large saucepan. Stir in the potato flakes until well blended. Reduce heat to low.

2. Place the peanut butter in a bowl and whisk in 1 cup of the hot broth mixture, blending until smooth. Stir the peanut butter mixture into the saucepan and add the celery salt, onion powder, and pepper to taste. Simmer 5 minutes to heat through and blend flavors.

3. Serve sprinkled with the chopped peanuts.

MAKES 4 SERVINGS

White Beans and Greens Soup

This homey soup makes a hearty and economical main dish. Stellini, the small star-shaped pasta, add a touch of whimsy, but you can substitute another small soup pasta, such as *acine de pepe* or *pastene* (or even ramen).

1. Heat the oil in a large pot over medium heat. Add the garlic and cook until fragrant, 30 seconds. Stir in the broth, beans, onion, marjoram, savory, red pepper flakes, and salt and pepper to taste.

2. Bring to a boil, add the pasta, then reduce heat to low and simmer until the pasta is tender, about 6 minutes. Stir in the spinach. Serve hot.

MAKES 4 SERVINGS

2 teaspoons olive oil
3 garlic cloves, minced
4 cups vegetable broth (see page 119)
1 (15.5-ounce) can cannellini or other white beans, drained
2 teaspoons dehydrated minced onion
1/2 teaspoon dried marjoram
1/4 teaspoon dried savory
1/4 teaspoon red pepper flakes
Salt and black pepper
1/2 cup stellini or other small soup pasta
1 (8-ounce) can spinach, drained or 1/2 cup dehydrated spinach (added when you add the pasta)

Emergency Gazpacho

Sometimes, even during an emergency, you just find yourself wishing for gazpacho. This quick and easy "salad soup" goes together in a flash. If you want to serve it as a main dish, just add a can of drained chickpeas or pinto beans.

1 (14.5-ounce) can diced tomatoes, finely chopped
1 (4-ounce) jar roasted red peppers, chopped
1 (4-ounce) can chopped mild green chiles, drained
1 garlic clove, finely minced
1 tablespoon dehydrated minced onion
2 tablespoons chopped capers
1 tablespoon red wine vinegar
1 tablespoon olive oil
3 cups tomato or vegetable juice
1/2 teaspoon celery salt
1 teaspoon dried parsley
1 teaspoon Tabasco (optional)

Combine all of the ingredients in a large bowl and serve. Pass Tabasco at the table for those who like an extra jolt of heat.

MAKES 4 SERVINGS

Black Bean Soup with a Whisper of Sherry

This satisfying soup is substantial enough to serve as a main course. Serve it with crackers or toasted bread for some crunch-appeal. To make it creamier, puree up to half of the soup solids in a food mill and return it to the pot. A fresh onion or carrot makes a good addition. If you have them, mince them finely and saute them in the oil first.

1. Heat the oil in a large pot over medium heat. Add garlic, and cook until fragrant, 30 seconds. Stir in the oregano and cumin, then add the chiles, black beans, and tomatoes.

2. Add the broth and season with celery salt and pepper to taste. Simmer for 15 minutes to heat through and allow flavors to develop. Just before serving, stir in the sherry.

MAKES 4 SERVINGS

2 teaspoons olive oil
2 garlic cloves, minced
1/2 teaspoon dried oregano
1/2 teaspoon ground cumin
1 (4-ounce) can chopped mild green chiles, drained
2 (15.5-ounce) cans black beans, drained
1 (14.5-ounce) can diced tomatoes, drained
4 cups vegetable broth (see page 119) or water
1/4 teaspoon celery salt, or to taste
Black pepper
2 tablespoons dry sherry

Shiitake Happens Mushroom Soup

Mushroom lovers will savor the rich flavor created by using a variety of mushrooms. Some people enjoy using dried mushrooms for their strong, earthy flavor. If you're not one of them, stick with the canned and jarred variety for a milder, yet still flavorful soup. To make this soup a meal, add a can of white beans.

1/4 ounce dried wild mushrooms
  or 1 (8-ounce) can straw
  mushrooms, drained
2 teaspoons olive oil
2 garlic cloves, minced
3 tablespoons dry sherry
1 tablespoon dehydrated minced
  onion
1/2 teaspoon dried thyme
4 cups vegetable broth (see page
  119)
1/2 cup quick-cooking rice
1 (10-ounce) jar sliced shiitake
  mushrooms, drained
1 (8-ounce) jar sliced button
  mushrooms, drained
1 teaspoon dried parsley
1/4 teaspoon celery salt
1/4 teaspoon black pepper

1. If using dried mushrooms, soak them in enough hot water to cover until softened. Thinly slice the mushrooms and set them aside. Save the soaking water.

2. Heat the oil in a large pot over medium heat. Add the garlic and cook until fragrant, 30 seconds. Stir in the sherry, onion, and thyme, and cook 1 minute longer.

3. If using dried mushrooms, add them to the pot along with the broth and 1/2 cup of the mushroom soaking water if you have it and bring to a boil. Reduce heat to low, add the rice, the straw mushrooms, if using, the shiitake and button mushrooms, parsley, celery salt, and pepper. Simmer for 10 minutes. Taste to adjust seasonings.

MAKES 4 SERVINGS

Instant Vichyssoise

The classic French version of this soup is served cold, but chilling it can be tricky without refrigeration. During the summer months, you can chill it in the ice chest, if you have ice. Otherwise, "room temperature" will be the new "chilled." To make a quick, hot potato soup instead, add a can of drained diced potatoes and heat it in a saucepan.

1. Bring the broth to a boil. Stir in the potato flakes, reduce heat to low, and simmer 5 minutes, stirring frequently. Remove from the heat and set aside to cool.

2. Stir in the non-dairy milk and season with salt and cayenne to taste. Serve the soup as chilled as is practical, sprinkled with the chives.

MAKES 4 SERVINGS

2 cups vegetable broth (see page 119)
1 cup instant potato flakes
2 cups non-dairy milk
Salt
Cayenne
1 tablespoon dried chives

Hot and Sour Soup

This ingenious soup does spicy, pungent, delicious, and soothing all in one bowl. It's also a great way to use those dried mushrooms and that aseptic box of silken tofu sitting in your pantry.

1/4 ounce dried cloud ear mushrooms or 1 (8-ounce) can straw mushrooms, drained
2 teaspoons canola oil
2 garlic cloves, minced
1 tablespoon grated ginger (optional)
4 cups vegetable broth (see page 119)
2 teaspoons dehydrated onion
3 tablespoons soy sauce
2 tablespoons rice vinegar
1/2 teaspoon sugar
1 teaspoon Asian chile paste
1 (8-ounce) can bamboo shoots, drained and cut into strips
2 teaspoons cornstarch dissolved in 1 tablespoon water
1 (12-ounce) aseptic package extra-firm tofu, cut into 1/4-inch dice
2 teaspoons toasted sesame oil
1 teaspoon Asian chili oil

1. If using dried mushrooms, soak them in a bowl of hot water until softened. Drain and cut into julienne strips and set aside.

2. Heat the canola oil in a large saucepan over medium heat. Add the garlic and ginger (if using) and cook until fragrant, about 30 seconds. Add the vegetable broth, onion, soy sauce, vinegar, sugar, chile paste, bamboo shoots, and the mushrooms. Bring to a boil over high heat, then reduce to a simmer and cook over medium heat for 5 minutes to allow the flavors to combine. Add the cornstarch mixture, stirring to thicken slightly.

3. Add the tofu, sesame oil, and chili oil, and cook until heated through, about 5 minutes.

MAKES 4 SERVINGS

Pretty Good Gumbo

The name of this spicy Cajun soup means "okra," although some people may choose not to include the mucilaginous vegetable when they make the soup. If you grew up in Louisiana, or have tasted a really good gumbo, this will put you in mind of better days. The optional filé powder is made from ground sassafras leaves and is available at gourmet grocers or online.

1. Heat the oil in a large pot over medium heat. Add the garlic and cook until fragrant, 30 seconds.

2. Stir in the tomatoes, bell pepper, onion, and broth and bring to a boil. Reduce heat to low and add the kidney beans, rice, okra (if using), thyme, filé powder (if using), celery salt, and salt and pepper to taste.

3. Simmer, stirring occasionally, until rice is tender and soup is hot, 5 minutes. Add the Tabasco and taste to adjust the seasonings. Serve hot.

MAKES 4 SERVINGS

2 teaspoons olive oil
2 garlic cloves, minced
1 (14.5-ounce) can diced tomatoes, drained
1 (6-ounce) jar roasted red bell pepper, diced
1 tablespoon dehydrated minced onion
6 cups vegetable broth (see page 119) or water
1 (15.5-ounce) can dark red kidney beans, drained
1/2 cup quick-cooking rice
1 (14-ounce) can okra, drained and sliced (optional)
1 teaspoon dried thyme
1 teaspoon filé powder (optional)
1/4 teaspoon celery salt
Salt and black pepper
1 teaspoon Tabasco, or to taste

Use-It-Up Minestrone Soup

The classic Italian vegetable soup is a good way to use up any fresh veggies or herbs you have on hand by swapping them out for the canned vegetables in this recipe. Just slice the fresh veggies as thin as possible so you can shorten cooking time. Dehydrated vegetables may also be used instead of (or in addition to) canned or fresh.

2 teaspoons olive oil
2 large garlic cloves, minced
1 (15.5-ounce) can chickpeas, drained
1 (14.5 ounce) can diced tomatoes, undrained
1 (8-ounce) can sliced carrots, drained
1 (8-ounce) can sliced zucchini, drained
1 (8-ounce) can cut green beans, drained
1 (6-ounce) jar roasted red bell peppers, drained and diced
4 cups vegetable broth (see page 119)
1 tablespoon dehydrated minced onion
1 teaspoon dried parsley
1 teaspoon dried basil
1/4 teaspoon dried oregano
Salt and black pepper

1. Heat the oil in a large saucepan over medium heat. Add the garlic and cook until fragrant, 30 seconds.

2. Stir in the chickpeas, tomatoes and their juice, carrots, zucchini, green beans, bell peppers, broth, and onion. Season with parsley, basil, oregano, and salt and pepper to taste. Bring to a boil, then reduce heat to low and simmer 15 minutes.

MAKES 4 SERVINGS

Curry-Spiced Pumpkin Bisque

If you're in the mood for a savory, creamy soup, this is as close as you're going to get from a canned-goods pantry. If you like the flavor combination of curry and pumpkin, you'll make this treat even after the lights come on.

1. Combine the pumpkin, curry powder, brown sugar, coriander, and cumin in a pot over medium heat. Whisk in the coconut milk a little at a time until smooth. Add up to a cup of the vegetable broth to achieve the desired consistency. Season with salt and pepper, to taste.

2. Simmer for 10 minutes to allow flavors to develop, stirring occasionally. Taste to adjust seasonings and serve hot, garnished with pumpkin seeds, if desired.

MAKES 4 SERVINGS

1 (15-ounce) can pumpkin puree
1 tablespoon curry powder
1 teaspoon light brown sugar
1/2 teaspoon ground coriander
1/4 teaspoon ground cumin
1 (15-ounce) can unsweetened coconut milk
1 cup vegetable broth (see page 119)
Salt and black pepper
2 tablespoons pumpkin seeds (optional garnish)

Comforting Corn Chowder

This sweet, satisfying chowder is made with a canned whole kernel corn. The optional garnish of pimiento will add a dash of color and can give the impression around the neighborhood that you've been doing this a long time.

2 (15-ounce) cans corn kernels, drained, or 1 cup dehydrated corn, rehydrated (page 34)
1 (15-ounce) can diced white potatoes, drained
1 tablespoon dehydrated minced onion
1/4 teaspoon celery salt
2 cups vegetable broth (see page 119)
1 cup non-dairy milk
1 tablespoon cornstarch combined with 2 tablespoons water
Black pepper
1 (2-ounce) jar chopped pimientos, drained (optional)

1. Combine the corn, potatoes, onion, celery salt, and broth in a large pot and bring to a boil. Reduce heat to medium and simmer, stirring frequently, for 5 minutes.

2. Add the non-dairy milk and return to a simmer. Stir in the cornstarch mixture and stir until thickened slightly. Season to taste with pepper.

3. Ladle the soup into bowls and garnish with pimientos, if using.

MAKES 4 SERVINGS

Artichoke, Shiitake, and White Bean Soup

So delicious, it's hard to believe how quick and easy this soup is to make. And with elegant ingredients like artichokes and shiitake mushrooms, you may forget for a moment that you're eating Pantry Cuisine.

1. Combine all the ingredients in a large pot and bring to a boil. Reduce heat to low and simmer to heat through and develop the flavor, about 10 minutes.

2. Remove the bay leaf before serving. Serve hot.

MAKES 4 SERVINGS

1 (14-ounce) can artichoke hearts, drained and chopped

1 (15.5-ounce) can Great Northern or other white beans, drained

1 (10-ounce) jar sliced shiitake mushrooms, drained or 1/2 cup dehydrated sliced shiitakes, rehydrated (page 34)

1 tablespoon dehydrated minced onion

4 cups vegetable broth (see page 119)

1 teaspoon dried savory

1 bay leaf

Salt, to taste

Cayenne pepper, to taste

Snack Food Chic

This chapter is about snacks. Not just any snacks, but snacks that will propel you beyond the potato chip-and-pretzel rut of your old life, into a new snack awareness. Would you believe Red Pepper Walnut Spread and a yummy tapenade? Even better than that, this chapter offers a fabulous version of "gorp" (good old raisins and peanuts) as an amuse bouche. You'll also discover some tasty comfort foods. They'll satisfy your hunger and also help relieve the stress, as you channel your energy into making an assortment of treats that are as much fun to make as they are to eat.

Savvy Snacking

Artichoke Dip

Gorp Redux

Chickpea Spread

Corn and Black Bean Salsa

Red Pepper-Walnut Spread

Texas Twister Caviar

Happy Trails Mix

Almond Stuffed Dates

Tapenade with Classy Crackers

Tropical Energy Balls

Peanutty Granola Balls

Artichoke Dip

This zesty dip is great served with crackers, chips, or bagel crisps.

1. Soak the sunflower seeds in hot water for 1 hour. Drain and set aside.

2. Use a hand chopper or grinder to finely mince the sunflower seeds and artichoke hearts. If you don't have a grinder or chopper, use a sharp knife. Transfer to a bowl.

3. Add a few drops of Tabasco and salt to taste. Mix well to incorporate. Taste to adjust seasonings.

MAKES 1 1/2 CUPS

1/4 cup sunflower seeds
1 (6-ounce) jar marinated artichoke hearts, drained
Tabasco

Gorp Redux

This is our signature gorp, or, more accurately, "gobacch," for "good old blueberries, almonds, cranberries, chocolate, and hazelnuts." If you're really bored, you can place two or three pieces of the mixture (a cranberry and two hazelnuts, for example) on salad plates and serve it as an *amuse bouche* before a meal.

1 cup vegan white chocolate
    chips
1 cup sweetened dried cranberries
1 cup sweetened dried blueberries
1 cup slivered almonds
1 cup hazelnuts

1. Combine all the ingredients in a large bowl. Toss gently to combine.

2. Divide mixture into 5 small resealable plastic food storage bags. Store in a cool dry place.

MAKES ABOUT 5 CUPS

GORP, A HISTORY

All backpackers know about gorp—"good old raisins and peanuts." It was the original trail mix, and variations have incorporated nuts and dried fruit combos with chocolate chips and other yummy ingredients.

Chickpea Spread

What's hummus without the tahini? It's this chickpea spread! Serve with crackers or chips for a high-protein snack.

Combine all the ingredients in a medium bowl. Use a potato masher or ricer to mash the chickpeas to a paste, then use a spoon to mix well, incorporating all the ingredients. Taste and adjust the seasonings, if needed.

MAKES ABOUT 2 CUPS

- 1 (15.5-ounce) can chickpeas, drained
- 2 tablespoons lemon juice
- 1 tablespoon olive oil
- 1/2 teaspoon garlic powder
- 1/4 teaspoon salt
- 1/8 teaspoon smoked paprika

Corn and Black Bean Salsa

This recipe combines three pantry ingredients to make a luscious bowl of salsa. Serve with a bag of corn chips and enjoy this nutrient-rich snack for dinner. Being unplugged never tasted so good.

Combine all the ingredients in a medium bowl. Mix well. Serve with chips.

MAKES ABOUT 3 CUPS

- 1 (8-ounce) jar mild or hot tomato salsa
- 1 (8-ounce) can corn kernels, drained
- 1 (15.5-ounce) can black beans, drained

Red Pepper-Walnut Spread

The hearty flavor of this vibrant spread is as yummy on crackers as it is on toasted bread.

1 cup chopped walnut pieces
1 teaspoon olive oil
1 garlic clove, minced
1 (6-ounce) jar roasted red bell
    peppers, drained
1 teaspoon dried parsley
1/2 teaspoon onion powder
Salt and black pepper

1. Finely grind the walnuts using a manual nut grinder or place in a plastic bag and crush them with a rolling pin or rubber mallet. Set aside.

2. Heat the oil in a small skillet over medium heat, add the garlic, cover, and cook until soft, about 1 minute. Transfer to a bowl.

3. Finely mince the roasted bell peppers and garlic using a manual food chopper or use a potato ricer or food mill to get the peppers as close to pureed as possible. Add the parsley, onion powder, reserved walnuts, and salt and pepper to taste. Stir well to combine. Transfer to a small serving bowl.

MAKES 4 SERVINGS

Texas Twister Caviar

Black-eyed peas are the featured ingredient in this satisfying spread. Serve it on crackers or use it as a tasty sandwich filling.

1. Place the black-eyed peas and tomatoes in a bowl and mash well. Stir in the garlic powder, onion powder, parsley, oil, vinegar, mustard, and cayenne.

2. Season to taste with salt and pepper to taste, and stir until well combined.

MAKES 4 SERVINGS

1 (15.5-ounce) can black-eyed peas, drained
1 (14.5-ounce) can diced tomatoes, drained
1/4 teaspoon garlic powder
1/4 teaspoon onion powder
1 tablespoon dried parsley
1 tablespoon olive oil
2 teaspoons cider vinegar
1/2 teaspoon dried mustard
1/4 teaspoon cayenne
Salt and black pepper

A DOUBLE-DUTY SNACK

Pistachios in the shell make a great snack food. They also give you something to do while the power is out, because you need to open each nut one at a time.

Happy Trails Mix

The combination of sweet and savory flavors and soft and crunchy textures makes this an ideal snack to perk you up in a variety of situations. Stash away an extra bag or two for when you need a healthy jolt. Seal your mix in airtight sandwich bags, and keep in a reasonably cool spot. It will stay fresh for several days. This recipe can be easily halved.

2 cups mini pretzels
2 cups dry-roasted peanuts
1 1/2 cups chocolate chips
1 1/2 cups dried cranberries
1 1/2 cups crispy cereal squares
1 1/2 cups sunflower seeds or
    pepitas (pumpkin seeds)

1. Combine all the ingredients in a large bowl. Toss gently to combine.

2. Divide mixture into 10 small resealable plastic food storage bags. Store in a cool dry place.

MAKES ABOUT 10 CUPS

Almond Stuffed Dates

Here's a nutritious and delicious snack recipe that requires just two ingredients and takes about 30 seconds to make.

12 almonds (raw, dry-roasted, or
    blanched)
12 pitted dates

Stuff an almond into each of the dates. Arrange on a plate. Devour.

MAKES 12

Tapenade with Classy Crackers

Although the name tapenade refers to the requisite capers with which it is normally made, the olives are really the star of the show. Oil-cured black olives have a deeper flavor than those cured in brine, but brine-cured can be used if they're all you've got. If you must, use regular canned supermarket olives, although they lack the rich flavor you want in a tapenade. We like to serve it with classy crackers like Bremner's Wafers or Carr's Table Water Crackers, but you can use any kind you prefer.

1. Heat the oil in a small skillet over medium heat. Add the garlic and cook until soft and fragrant, about 30 seconds.

2. In a bowl combine the garlic, olives, capers, parsley, and salt. Mix together until the mixture is thoroughly blended. Transfer to a small bowl and serve with crackers.

MAKES 1 CUP

NOTE: For those times when you don't feel like making your own, commercially prepared jars of tapenade are available at well-stocked supermarkets and gourmet grocers. Once opened, it must be used up or stored on ice.

2 teaspoons olive oil
1 garlic clove run through a garlic press
1 cup pitted oil-cured black olives, minced
2 tablespoons capers, drained
1 teaspoon dried parsley
1/2 teaspoon salt
Crackers of choice

Tropical Energy Balls

When a storm zaps your power, try these yummy treats for a taste of the tropics.

1 cup pitted dates or mixed dried
    fruit
1 cup walnut pieces
1/2 cup flaked coconut (plus more
    for rolling balls, if using)
1 tablespoon almond butter or
    other nut butter
1/2 teaspoon vanilla extract

1. Soak the dates or fruit in a bowl of warm water for 15 minutes.

2. While the fruit is soaking, use a hand chopper, knife, or rubber mallet to finely chop the nuts. Place the nuts in a bowl and add the coconut, almond butter, and vanilla. Incorporate with a pastry blender.

3. Coat a pair of scissor blades with non-stick cooking spray and snip the dates or fruit into the nut mixture with the scissors. Use the pastry blender or your hands to blend the mixture together.

4. Use your hands to shape the mixture into balls. Roll in additional coconut, if desired.

MAKES ABOUT 16

Peanutty Granola Balls

Like a bite-sized granola bar, these tasty bites make terrific energy-boosting between-meal snacks. They also make a fun, hassle-free breakfast.

1. Combine the peanut butter, maple syrup, and juice in a bowl and use a pastry blender to mix until well blended.

2. Stir in the granola and mix well. Use your hands to roll the mixture into 1-inch balls and arrange on a plate. Roll in crushed peanuts, if desired.

MAKES ABOUT 12

- 1/4 cup peanut butter
- 2 tablespoons maple syrup
- 2 tablespoons apple juice (or other fruit juice)
- 1 1/2 cups granola
- 1/2 cup finely crushed peanuts or other nuts (optional)

Just Desserts

This chapter provides easy recipes for great homemade desserts made from your on-hand stash. Some of them are even healthy, though one doesn't often mention health in the same sentence as dessert.

Some of these recipes call for fruit, and you can use canned or dried. Hopefully you stocked up on both. If you still have fresh fruit on hand, save them to enjoy as a snack. You get more nutrients that way and can enjoy the true flavor and texture of the fruit uncomplicated by sugar and spice. If you tire of noshing on dried fruit, simmer them in sugar water for a lovely fruit *macédoine* that can be enjoyed for dessert or as a special topping for oatmeal or pancakes.

Dessert Every Day

Instant Gratification Chocolate Pie

Strawberry Needles in White Chocolate Haystacks

Darling Clementines with Pistachios and Cranberries

Skillet Peach Crumble

Fire-Roasted Blueberry Cobbler

No-Fuss Chocolate Fondue

Sweet Treat Chocolate Truffles

Ginger-Walnut Rum Balls

Pears and Peanuts with a Flourish of Chocolate

Instant Gratification Chocolate Pie

You want chocolate pie, and you want it now. But when there's no oven for baking and no refrigerator for chilling, this decadent dessert is a good bet. Note: If you don't have a vegan chocolate cookie crust, finely crush vegan cookies to equal 1 1/2 cups of crumbs.

1. Melt the chocolate chips in a metal bowl over a saucepan of simmering water. Cook, stirring until the chocolate is melted.

2. Stir the cookie crust crumbs into the melted chocolate. Add the walnuts, dried fruit, and coconut and mix until well combined.

3. Transfer the chocolate mixture to a pie pan and spread evenly, using your fingers, if necessary, to press the mixture into the pan. Set aside to firm up before serving.

12 ounces vegan semisweet chocolate chips
1 vegan chocolate cookie crust, finely crumbled (Keebler brand is vegan-friendly)
3/4 cup chopped walnuts
3/4 cup dried cherries, cranberries, and golden raisins (in any combination)
3/4 cup shredded coconut, firmly packed

MAKES 8 SERVINGS

THERAPY ON A PLATE

I think of dessert as therapy on a plate because sweets are the ultimate comfort food. Even the experts agree that during emergency situations, sweets are a good idea to help relieve stress. After all, "stressed" is "desserts" spelled backwards. It can't be a coincidence.

Strawberry Needles
in White Chocolate Haystacks

Finding a needle in a haystack was never so tasty. An unlikely quartet of ingredients? Sure, but wait until you taste them!

1 piece strawberry fruit leather
8 ounces vegan white chocolate
1/2 cup toasted slivered almonds
1 1/2 cups chow mein noodles

1. Use a pair of kitchen shears to cut the fruit leather into extremely fine strips, less than 1/16-inch thick. Set aside.

2. Melt the white chocolate in a metal bowl over a saucepan of simmering water.

3. When the chocolate is melted, stir in the almonds, noodles, and reserved fruit leather "needles." Mix well.

4. While still warm, use a teaspoon to drop the mixture into small mounds onto a baking sheet lined with parchment paper or waxed paper. (You can use your hands to create more haystack-like shapes, if you like). Set aside to firm up.

MAKES ABOUT 24

Darling Clementines
with Pistachios and Cranberries

Admittedly, canned fruit pales by comparison to fresh, but you'll be surprised how good this tastes. Pour on a splash of fragrant orange flower water, a sprinkle of pistachios, dried cranberries, and finish with a sprig of mint, and you've elevated this canned fruit to a gorgeous gourmet treat. Try this same treatment on canned apricots, peaches, or mandarin oranges.

1. Arrange the clementines in a bowl with 1/4 cup of its liquid. Sprinkle with pistachios and cranberries.

2. Splash with the orange flower water and lemon juice, if using. Garnish with mint leaves, if available.

MAKES 4 SERVINGS

Note: Orange flower water is distilled from orange blossoms and is available at gourmet markets.

2 (8-ounce) cans clementine orange segments, drained (reserve 1/4 cup liquid)
1/4 cup chopped pistachio nuts
2 tablespoons sweetened dried cranberries
2 teaspoons orange flower water (optional)
1 teaspoon lemon juice (optional)
Mint leaves (from your garden or windowsill, if available optional)

Skillet Peach Crumble

Similar to a fruit crisp, this dessert is made in a skillet on a stovetop instead of in the oven. The basis of the "crumble" topping is healthful, toothsome oats. Yum. It's also great made with apple or blueberry pie filling and can be a go-to dessert even when you're plugged in but don't feel like heating up the oven.

2/3 cup old-fashioned or quick-cooking oats
1/4 cup light brown sugar or a natural sweetener
1 tablespoon peanut butter
1 tablespoon canola oil
1 teaspoon ground cinnamon
1/8 teaspoon salt
1 (28-ounce) can sliced peaches, drained

1. In a medium bowl, combine the oats, sugar, peanut butter, oil, cinnamon, and salt. Mix well and cook in a 10-inch skillet over medium heat until toasted, stirring frequently to avoid burning, about 5 minutes. Scrape topping mixture back into the bowl.

2. In the same skillet, spread the peach slices in the same direction in concentric rows. Sprinkle the reserved topping on top of the fruit.

3. Cover and cook over low heat until hot, about 10 minutes.

MAKES 4 SERVINGS

Fire-Roasted Blueberry Cobbler

It sounds improbable, but you can make a darn good cobbler over an open flame. The heat bubbles up through the filling to cook the cake-like topping. Keeping a lid closed tightly retains the heat. In a matter of minutes, you can have a fresh hot cobbler.

1. Combine the pie filling, cinnamon, and lemon juice or zest in a 10-inch skillet and place over a medium flame.

2. In a bowl, combine the flour, sugar, baking powder, and salt. Stir in the non-dairy milk and oil, mixing until just combined.

3. Spread the batter evenly over the blueberry mixture. Cover and cook until the batter becomes firm and cake-like, about 15 minutes. Turn off heat and let stand covered for another 5 to 10 minutes.

MAKES 4 SERVINGS

1 (21-ounce) can blueberry pie filling
1 pinch cinnamon
1 teaspoon lemon juice or lemon zest
1 cup all-purpose flour
1/3 cup sugar
1 teaspoons baking powder
1 pinch salt
1/2 cup non-dairy milk
2 tablespoons canola oil

No-Fuss Chocolate Fondue

Fondue is easy to assemble, fun to eat, and delicious in the bargain. What better way to while away the hours than by dipping chunks of cake, cookies, fruit, and pretzels into a pot of warm rich chocolate laced with your favorite liqueur?

8 ounces vegan semi-sweet chocolate
1/2 cup non-dairy milk
3 tablespoons sugar
1 to 2 tablespoons liqueur of choice (optional, Frangelico, Amaretto, Drambuie, etc.)

Dippers:
Assorted fresh, canned, or reconstituted dried fruit for dipping, cut into bite-size pieces as necessary
Vegan cake or cookies, cut into bite-sized pieces
Pretzel sticks

1. Break the chocolate into pieces and place in a fondue pot. Light the Sterno, cover, and stir the chocolate occasionally until melted.

2. Blend in the non-dairy milk and sugar. Stir in the liqueur, if using. Cover and let the mixture continue to heat until the chocolate mixture is hot. (Note: If you don't have a fondue pot, melt the chocolate mixture in a metal bowl over a saucepan of simmering water. You can leave it in the bowl to serve.)

3. Arrange the "dippers" on plates and set them on the table with fondue forks or wooden skewers. Let everyone dig in.

MAKES 4 TO 6 SERVINGS

Sweet Treat Chocolate Truffles

In a perfect world, you would refrigerate these little beauties for a while, just to help them firm up. But they are still amazingly delicious without chilling and the peanuts keep them from sticking to your fingers.

1. Melt the chocolate in a metal bowl over a saucepan of simmering water.

2. Remove from heat and stir in the sugar and peanut butter, mixing until well combined.

3. Use your hands to shape the mixture into 1-inch balls and set on a plate lined with plastic film wrap.

4. Roll the balls in the crushed peanuts and set aside in a cool spot if possible to firm up a bit.

MAKES 10 TO 12

1/2 cup vegan semi-sweet chocolate chips
1/2 cup confectioners' sugar
1/4 cup peanut butter
1/3 cup finely crushed dry-roasted peanuts

Ginger-Walnut Rum Balls

The best thing about this recipe, in addition to getting to drink the leftover rum, is that no heat or refrigeration is needed to make them. In fact, they benefit from sitting out at room temperature. If you're not a fan of ginger snaps, substitute another type of cookie. To finely crush the walnuts, enclose them in a plastic bag and gently roll over them several times with a rolling pin or wine bottle or rubber mallet. For a non-alcoholic version, use apple juice in place of the rum.

1 cup finely crushed vegan gingersnap crumbs

1/2 cup plus 1/4 cup confectioners' sugar

1/4 cup finely crushed walnuts

2 tablespoons dark rum

2 tablespoons maple syrup

1. In a bowl, combine cookie crumbs, 1/2 cup of the confectioners' sugar, the ground nuts, rum, and maple syrup. Use your hands to mix together thoroughly until the mixture holds together.

2. Shape the mixture into 1-inch balls. Roll the balls in remaining 1/4 cup confectioners' sugar and arrange on a plate. Cover with plastic film wrap and let sit for several hours or overnight to allow flavors to develop.

MAKES 18

Pears and Peanuts
with a Flourish of Chocolate

This is a great way to enjoy canned pears and a nice change from slurping them off your fingers. If you have fresh ripe pears, you can use them instead of canned.

1. Cut the pears into bite-sized chunks and transfer to a serving bowl or individual dessert dishes. Sprinkle the nuts on top.

2. Use a vegetable peeler to make chocolate curls out of the chocolate bar. Top the pears and peanuts with the chocolate and serve.

1 (28-ounce) can pear halves, drained
1/2 cup crushed dry-roasted peanuts
1 bar vegan semisweet baking chocolate (or vegan chocolate candy bar)

MAKES 4 SERVINGS

THINK FRUIT

Instead of sulking because you can't make a batch of your favorite cupcakes, think fruit. Many fruits actually hold up well at room temperature. Plan ahead to keep on hand a supply of apples, firm pears, green bananas (so they ripen slowly), and citrus fruit, among others. They can be delicious and fun to eat, either out of hand or cut-up and served in a glass bowl.

12

Emergency Preparedness Guide

It doesn't take much to upset the U.S. power grid. Hurricanes, floods, earthquakes, tornadoes, wild fires, ice, snow, wind storms, and even thunderstorms regularly knock out the power. So, while you may be enjoying Pantry Cuisine under ordinary circumstances, it will be your best choice when you fall victim to manmade emergencies. These range from blackouts and brownouts to events sponsored by Mother Nature.

A power outage can last hours, days, weeks, or longer. Just ask the Floridians who endured four hurricanes in 2004, or Gulf Coast residents, some of whom still live with the aftermath of Hurricane Katrina. Midwesterners suffered a week

and more without power after region-wide January ice storms in both 2009 and 2010.

We are walking, talking electricity addicts, so losing our electricity plunges us into situations in which we are sometimes unable to communicate, travel, bathe, or eat properly. With your refrigerator out of commission, your perishable food spoils in a couple of days, your frozen in three. If your home is all-electric, you are out of luck—unless you're prepared.

After disasters, natural gas is often turned off for safety reasons, and tap water can become undrinkable. After three days without heat, air conditioning, or stove, a power outage can also turn the lambs among us into beasts. No one is exempt. It's just a matter of time before any of us find ourselves living as our ancestors once did—sweating (or shivering) without refrigeration and wishing we had decent food to eat.

To cope with it all, this chapter concisely explains how to prepare for emergencies and how to deal with mandatory evacuations. Chapter 13 details how to safeguard your animal companions in the event of an emergency. Chapter 14 offers helpful and creative ways to cope with the stress and make the best of it.

> ### GETTING 'READY'
>
> Visit www.ready.gov, the U.S. Department of Homeland Security Web site, for advice on natural disasters and planning kits.

The Time to Plan Is Now

As you'll see below, a variety of forces can threaten our power supply, and *Vegan Unplugged* provides guidelines for those situations. However, even though you are likely to be visited by one or more of them during your lifetime, hope glimmers like a flame beneath a chafing dish, and its name is Be Prepared. You have already packed your Five-Day Meal Box and stashed it away with your single-burner butane stove. You have stocked your Pantry Stash and become familiar with Pantry Cuisine. You already know the order in which to use up your fresh and frozen foods, and, in so doing, have won half the battle of surviving well in an emergency. The other half requires a Disaster Supply List and a Family Plan.

The Evacuation Dilemma

If your power goes out because of some technical glitch, such as a blackout, odds are you won't have to evacuate your home. In the case of a tornado, you won't have enough warning to evacuate. Likewise for earthquakes. But with an approaching hurricane, flood, or wildfire, authorities can track the direction and evacuation orders boil down to two possibilities: they can urge evacuation by way of a "warning," or they can order a mandatory evacuation. This book urges you to do as the authorities ask, their concern is for your safety and health as well as the safety of rescue officials who may have to come rescue you. Whether you entrench inside your home or get out of Dodge, there are things you can do to prepare—precautions that you will be glad you took.

> ### FILL 'ER UP
>
> Without power, you can't pump gasoline. Therefore, it's a good idea to fill up prior to any approaching storm. You can also siphon gas from the car to use in the generator.

Mandatory Evacuation

When officials order you to evacuate, it's best to have a plan, or at the last minute you may find yourself drawing a blank on what to take with you. If the situation is bad, you will wish you had taken at least as much as would fit in your car. If you wait until the storm arrives, it's too late, because this type of planning takes time and thought.

So, well before a major loss of power hits your area, do what we recently did at our house: assemble a Disaster Supply Kit, like the National Weather Service tells you. This box is a centralized cache of your most important papers and other things that you may need quick access to, whether you stay home or flee from danger. Ours is a plastic storage box (a special container additional to our Five-Day Meal Box) with a snug snap-on lid that can be quickly loaded into the trunk of the car. It contains the documents and other items that will ensure our fiscal and legal future, should our house be partially or completely destroyed. When we lived in Virginia Beach, this was highly probable, as we lived only three blocks from the Atlantic Ocean.

COMPUTER USERS

Back up your hard disk regularly, but make a special backup if you have warning of a coming calamity. Store the backup with your Disaster Supply Kit.

In this box, you will keep an envelope with the records you'll need to prove you haven't been "disappeared" by some black-ops secret agency: birth and marriage certificates, passports, insurance papers, bank books, investment records, wills, medical documents, vaccination records for children and companion animals (more on that in the next chapter), any other legal papers, and space for the address book and other truly last-minute items. (See the complete Disaster Supply Kit list on page 161.) You will also include photocopies of recent utility bills—electric, phone, water, etc.—so you can contact these utilities with your account numbers.

The box should also contain a set of your phone directories in case you need to make calls to local businesses before you can return. We regularly burn complete computer backups onto DVDs or jump drives; these would be added at the last minute. A laptop would also fit in this box. Because we conduct our business with computers, we would reserve car space for the CPUs, if not the monitors. In the bottom of this box, we keep that single-burner butane stove with some extra fuel.

Disaster Supply Kit

Whenever you are forced to leave your home, take with you as many items on this list as you can:

- Water – at least 1 gallon daily per person for 3 to 7 days
- Food – enough for 3 to 7 days; non-perishable foods/juices
- Specialty items for infants or the elderly
- Snack food
- Cooking tools – manual can opener, stove and fuel, saucepan, plates, utensils, etc.
- Blankets, pillows, etc.
- Clothing – seasonal, rain gear, sturdy shoes
- First Aid kit, medicines, prescription drugs
- Toiletries, hygiene items, moisture wipes
- Flashlight, batteries
- Radio – battery operated and NOAA weather radio
- Cash – banks and ATMs may be closed or only available for limited periods
- Keys
- Toys, books, and games
- Important documents – keep insurance, medical records, bank account numbers, Social Security card, etc., in a waterproof container

- Tools – keep a compact set of hand tools with you during the storm

- Fuel – make sure you fill your vehicle fuel tanks before the storm hits

- Pet care items – proper identification, immunization records, medications; ample supply of food and water; a carrier or cage; leash; litter box, litter, and scoop

- Hand sanitizer (minimum 60% alcohol content)

- Solar cell phone charger

- Lamps; lamp oil; matches in waterproof container

(ADAPTED FROM THE NATIONAL HURRICANE CENTER OF THE NATIONAL WEATHER SERVICE.)

For information on ways in which you can strengthen your home for resistance to damage in violent storms, see the National Hurricane Center Web site, www.nhc.noaa.gov/HAW2/english/intro.shtml.

Choosing Not to Evacuate?

If the authorities have not requested or ordered you to leave your home, then you may elect to ride out the event inside your house. If you so choose, you can take steps to keep safe and guarantee some basic comforts to get you through the aftermath. The National Weather Service suggests every household to make a Family Disaster Plan (residents of Florida and North Carolina's Outer Banks are well acquainted with this). Here you assess the vulnerability of your home, retrofit your house for safety, and make sure everyone knows the procedure when you're in harm's way. The plan makes sense for anyone, even those who don't live in a disaster-prone area.

Create a Family Plan

- Discuss the types of hazards that could affect your family. Know your home's vulnerability to storm surge, flooding, and wind

- Locate a safe room or the safest area in your home

- Determine escape routes from your home and places to rendezvous

- Have an out-of-state friend as a family contact, so all your family members have a single point of contact

- Make a plan now for what to do with your pets if you need to evacuate

- Post emergency telephone numbers by your phones and make sure your children know how to call 911

- Check your insurance coverage—flood damage is often not covered by homeowners insurance

- Stock non-perishable emergency supplies and a Disaster Supply Kit

- Use a NOAA weather radio. Remember to replace its battery every 6 months

- Take First Aid, CPR, and disaster preparedness classes

(COURTESY OF THE NATIONAL HURRICANE CENTER OF THE NATIONAL WEATHER SERVICE.)

After you have meticulously fulfilled the National Weather Service (NWS) checklist, you will be almost as prepared as possible to weather, say, a hurricane. Tucked securely in your safe room—a protected spot away from any windows—

you will keep your Disaster Supply Kit nearby, your Family Plan, and your Five-Day Meal Box. Unless the hurricane stalls over your house—and it can—it usually passes over and out of the picture in several hours. Once it's gone, you will venture outside, that is, if you aren't already outside. Even if you are not injured or worse, or if your house is wrecked and unlivable, you may be deeply sorry you didn't evacuate. All services will be out—electricity, possibly the water supply, fire services, ambulance, police, and maybe even the phones. In this situation, you must be extra careful not to hurt yourself. Stay off the roof, don't walk around barefoot. Be cautious with knives and other sharp objects.

But if all you've lost is your electrical power, as is the case with most people after such storms, you will start looking for another kit—your Five-Day Food Box meal supply kit, which will contain the items you need for cooking meals that not only taste great with a minimum of effort, but relieve the monotony of living life in the style of Lewis and Clark. Remember that this meal box is your meal ticket, whether you're stuck without power for emergency or non-emergency reasons. You will be glad you have it.

Following are case examples of the fragility of our power grid and a sensible guide to various emergency scenarios and what you need to know about them in order to be prepared.

TOP SAFETY TIPS FOR A BLACKOUT

- Use battery or solar-powered flashlights. Never candles!
- Turn off any electrical equipment in use when the power went out
- Avoid opening the refrigerator and freezer
- Don't run generators inside a home or garage
- Leave one light on so you know when the power returns
- Listen to local radio and television

(COURTESY OF THE AMERICAN RED CROSS, WWW.REDCROSS.ORG/SERVICES/DISASTER/0,1082,0_133_,00.HTML)

Unnatural Disasters

Mother Nature can knock out your power in a number of ways. Add the element of human bungling, however, and you know that the power grid can go down in any part of the country from California to New England and from Florida to Texas. Since you never know where you might end up living, it's wise to gain an overview of the various ways by which you can find yourself looking for nonperishable recipes.

Blackouts

If you think your electric stove is safe from natural disasters just because you don't live on the coast or in Tornado Alley, think again. Just consider our shaky power grid. In 2001, the California Power Crisis threw that state into rolling blackouts, the blame pinned on greedy market manipulators. North America's worst blackout, the 2003 U.S.-Canada Blackout, in which New York State lost 85 percent of its power, was caused by the Ohio equivalent of Mrs. O'Leary's cow. Former New Mexico governor, Bill Richardson, who is also a former head of the Department of Energy, once characterized the United States as "a superpower with a third-world electricity grid." More grid trouble lies ahead, say the experts, until we have the will to build a modern, efficient power grid like they have in Europe.

Blackouts, and even rolling brownouts, don't usually last very long. But, unlike hurricanes, winter storms, and floods, they can come without warning. Major East Coast blackouts occurred in 1965, 1977, 1987 (in New England, during the Great Storm), and several other occasions. Then we had the March 1989 Hydro-Québec outage: 6 million people had no electricity for nine hours. That may not sound so bad, until you consider the cause: a geo-magnetic storm from the sun— for these storms, there's no use packing an umbrella. Scientists tell us that magnetic interference from the sun increases every year. I don't particularly like to think about that.

Natural Disasters

Humankind, as we all know, can screw up anything, but for the really big block-busters, no one outdoes Mother Nature. As you will see, no one is excluded from her generosity.

Hurricanes

Hurricanes are as common on the coasts as bungalows. We remember the names: Katrina (2005), Isabel (2003), Floyd (1999), Andrew (1992), Hugo (1989), Agnes (1972), and Camille (1969), and dozens more that have made landfall in the U.S. since 1900. Between two and four of these tempests churn up the coast each year, often costing lives and always costing millions if not billions of dollars.

However lethal and damaging they are, hurricanes invariably leave survivors without power for anywhere from a few days to a few weeks. In 2004, many Floridians endured prolonged power outages as a result of four direct hits; Charley, Frances, Ivan, and Jeanne, all within six weeks. The aftermath of Hurricane Katrina on the Gulf Coast is painfully well known the world over.

In the event of evacuation, unless your destination has a working kitchen, you will appreciate having some basic kitchen items to prepare meals while you're away. Before you leave, you will want to grab your Five-Day Meal Box and Disaster Preparedness Kit. Naturally, if you'll be cooking at home, these items will already be within reach. However, in the event of evacuation, having everything in one place and ready to go will save you time at the last minute and come in handy.

Meteorological phenomena take the prize as the most dangerous quirks of nature, but the power grid can be interrupted regionally in various other ways. A thunderstorm can knock out power to a town or village, while the burg down the road is perfectly fine. This can happen anywhere, but Nor'easters (circular storms formed at sea that can't be promoted to hurricanes) plague the East Coast several times a year. And there are lots more.

Tornadoes

Tornadoes are quite different from hurricanes, because they give little warning, although the result is the same for survivors wherever power is lost. According to the National Weather Service Storm Prediction Center, the yearly average of tornadoes from 2002-2005 was 1,195, and they take the lives of an average of 49 people per year. From 2001 to 2004, 23 tornadoes that resulted in the loss of life were recorded in the U.S. A hurricane tears to pieces everything in its path; however, tornadoes seem to discriminate—they hop around, they come and go, and can devastate the block down the street while leaving your house untouched.

Twisters are a big problem in the Midwest, but you don't have to live down the lane from Auntie Em to find yourself in the path of one. Big brother and sister hurricanes spawn tornadoes as they spin, which often create some portion of the overall damage caused by hurricanes.

> ### BATHTUB WISDOM
>
> With a big storm approaching, fill your bathtub with water. That way, if municipal water shuts off, you can still wash dishes, wash yourself, and flush the toilet.

Think quickly when a tornado is in your area. Prepare in advance a place to hide, preferably the basement, or get under heavy furniture in the center of the house. Stay away from windows, though you should have the windows open, so your 3 BR, 2BA ranch w/AC doesn't implode. If you are in open country, lie flat in a ditch, ravine, or culvert. Also, be glad you made the Disaster Supply Kit and Family Plan described in this chapter.

Winter Storms

From southern to northern climes, winter storms regularly knock out power. Northern transmission line equipment tends to be tougher than that in the South; however, Easterners won't soon forget what was called Snowmageddon in the winter of 2010, when Washington, D.C., for one city among many, received two two-foot snowfalls within as many weeks. Hundreds of thousands were without power from North Carolina to New England. A big plus with a snowstorm is that your backyard now becomes your refrigerator for frozen foods, as long as the temperature remains below freezing, and below forty degrees for the rest. Just be sure to protect any food you store outside from wild animals, because their food will be covered by the snow and yours will appear to be a generous gift.

The next time an ice storm or blizzard plunges you into the deep freeze, you'll be prepared if you have:

- Fresh batteries in the house
- Backup for stored water and nonperishable food
- Protective clothing, mittens, boots
- Blankets and sleeping bags
- Snow shovel and salt
- Full tank of gas
- A heat source

Earthquakes

Most earthquakes in the U.S. are relatively small; however, there are precautions one can take. Unless you live in a sturdy old house, it's best to stay away from doorways when the temblor begins to shake. This is because modern construction, including doorways, are flimsy, and swinging doors can hurt you. Instead, duck beneath a heavy piece of furniture. (For further information on preparing for earthquakes, see: http://earthquake.usgs.gov/hazards/prepare.html.)

The U.S. Geological Survey National Earthquake Information Center states that between 2000 and 2003, two quakes had a magnitude of 7.0-7.9; 27 quakes had a magnitude of 7.0-7.9; and 231 quakes hit 6.0-6.9. Quakes registering 5.9 and below are ranked in categories from "moderate" to "very minor." Still, scientists continue to predict a powerful long-overdue earthquake for the West Coast.

After a quake, setting up your grill in the backyard may be the farthest thing from your mind. However, with the more common temblors and an accompanying power outage, preparation and the Five-Day Meal Box could spare you and your family a great deal of unnecessary hardship.

Epidemic or Pandemic?

In 2009, the H1N1 flu scare looked to be the pandemic to watch for. Analysis and vaccine production dragged on. Deaths were reported, but the disease mysteriously peaked and seemed to disappear, at least from the news reports.

In an epidemic, the germ spreads rapidly through a population, whereas, in a pandemic, the germ covers a wide geographical area (say, the world), infecting large segments of those populations. In either case, if we ever get into another situation like the Flu Epidemic of 1917, you may eventually find yourself using the food solutions in this book.

> ### THE SURVIVALIST'S "RULE OF THREE"
>
> The average human being can last:
> - 3 minutes without air
> - 3 days without water
> - 3 weeks without food

The reason is clear: If towns and cities go into quarantine mode, people will be forbidden to congregate in public places. But short of that, when the contagions are rapidly spreading, smart people will avoid restaurants and grocery stores as much as possible. If your home is free of infection, you may want to dip into your pantry supplies to gain another week without having to go out.

The U.S. Department of Health and Human Services (http://www.hhs.gov/) recommends frequent and thorough hand washing, preferably with hot water for the span of time it takes to sing Happy Birthday twice. If hot water isn't available, you can still wash your hands with soap in clean, running water. Absent hot water, an alcohol based (60% minimum) hand sanitizer is a must.

Following is a handy check list that can help keep us all safer from air-borne illness:

- Cough into the crook of your elbow

- Wash your hands frequently during the day

- Use an alcohol-based hand sanitizer (60%)

Food Safety During an Emergency

Did you know that a loss of electrical power could jeopardize the safety of your food? Knowing how to determine if food is safe and keep it safe will help minimize the potential loss of food and reduce the risk of food-borne illness. The following information from the USDA will help you make the right choices for keeping your family's food safe during an emergency.

ABCD's of Keeping Food Safe in an Emergency

Keep the refrigerator and freezer doors closed as much as possible to maintain the cold temperature. The refrigerator will keep food safely cold for about 4 hours if it is unopened. A full freezer will hold the temperature for approximately 48 hours (24 hours if it is half full) if the door remains closed. Plan ahead and know where block ice can be purchased.

Be prepared for an emergency by having items on hand that don't require refrigeration and can be eaten cold or heated on the outdoor grill. Shelf-stable food, boxed or canned non-dairy milks, water, and canned goods should be part of a planned emergency food supply. Be sure you have ready-to-use baby formula for infants and pet food. Remember to use these items and replace them from time to time. Be sure to keep a hand-held can opener for an emergency.

Consider what you can do ahead of time to store your food safely in an emergency. If you live in a location that could be affected by a flood, plan your food storage on shelves that will be safely out of the way of contaminated water. Coolers are a great help for keeping food cold if the power will be out for more than 4 hours—have a couple on hand along with frozen gel packs. When your freezer is not full, keep items close together—this helps the food stay cold longer.

Digital, dial, or instant-read food thermometers and appliance thermometers will help you know if the food is at safe temperatures. Keep appliance thermometers in the refrigerator and freezer at all times. When the power is out, an appliance thermometer will always indicate the temperature in the refrigerator and freezer no matter how long the power has been out. The refrigerator temperature should be 40°F or below; the freezer, 0°F or lower. If you're not sure a particular food is cold enough, take its temperature with a food thermometer.

(FOR MORE INFORMATION, VISIT THE U.S. DEPARTMENT OF AGRICULTURE FOOD SAFETY AND INSPECTION SERVICE WEB SITE: HTTP://WWW.FSIS.USDA.GOV/FACTSHEETS/KEEPING_FOOD_SAFE_DURING_AN_EMERGENCY/INDEX.ASP.)

In the following chapter, you will find general advice for caring for animal companions during and after an emergency. It includes the provisions of the PETS Act and FEMA's recommendations for taking care of the critters we love.

13

The Animals Need a Plan, Too

Whether you're staying home or leaving, make sure you plan for your compan-ion animals. Well in advance of any storm, bring your animals indoors—reassure them and help them to remain calm. If at all possible, keep your animals with you during a disaster.

If you need to evacuate, animals should not be left alone in the house. If for some reason you are unable to take your animals with you, try to plan ahead for a safe refuge, such as a specialized animal shelter, a veterinary clinic, or with friends and relatives who live out of harm's way.

Among the things to assemble for your animals in case of emergency are: proper identification collars and rabies tags, proper identification on all belongings, a carrier or cage, a leash, an ample supply of food and water, and bowls, any necessary medications clearly labeled, newspapers or trash bags, and/or litter and litter box.

The Homeland Preparedness online company (www.homelandpreparedness. com) and www.QuakeKare.com sell emergency survival kits for cats and dogs. (See Resources). These kits are packaged in waterproof containers and contain food, water, first-aid, sanitation, and shelter supplies for your cats or dogs. Check them out for ideas on how to create your own emergency survival kit for your animal companions.

THE PETS ACT

Hurricane Katrina exposed the catastrophic impact of failing to include animals in emergency planning. In October 2006, after recognizing the importance of including animals in emergency plans, President George W. Bush signed the Federal Pet Evacuation and Transportation Standards (PETS) Act into law. The law requires that state and local emergency plans address the needs of individuals with household pets and service animals. It also provides reimbursement to state and local governments for eligible pet evacuation and sheltering activities following a major disaster or emergency. Many states passed additional legislation to address the needs of animals including safety precautions for farm animals and horses.

(FROM THE HUMANE SOCIETY OF THE UNITED STATES WEBSITE: HTTP://WWW.HSUS.ORG/LEGISLATION_LAWS/FEDERAL_LEGISLATION/COMPANION_ANIMALS/PETS_ACT_SIGNED.HTML)

FEMA publishes a thorough checklist to plan for your animals in the event of a disaster. It is called "Information for Pet Owners" and the entire text follows:

FEMA Disaster Preparedness Checklist for Pets

If you evacuate your home, DO NOT LEAVE YOUR PETS BEHIND! Pets most likely cannot survive on their own. If by some remote chance they do, you may not be able to find them when you return. For additional information, contact The Humane Society of the United States.

Plan for Pet Disaster Needs

- Identifying shelter. For public health reasons, many emergency shelters cannot accept pets. Find out which motels and hotels in the area you plan to evacuate to allow pets—well in advance of needing them. There are also a number of guides that list hotels/motels that permit pets and could serve as a starting point. Include your local animal shelter's number in your list of emergency numbers—they might be able to provide information concerning pets during a disaster.
- Take pet food, bottled water, medications, veterinary records, cat litter/pan, can opener, food dishes, first aid kit and other supplies with you in case they're not available later. While the sun is still shining, consider packing a "pet survival" kit which could be easily deployed if disaster hits.
- Make sure identification tags are up to date and securely fastened to your pet's collar. If possible, attach the address and/or phone number of your evacuation site. If your pet gets lost, his tag is his ticket home. Make sure you have a current photo of your pet for identification purposes.
- Make sure you have a secure pet carrier, leash or harness for your pet so that if he panics, he can't escape.

Prepare to Shelter Your Pet

- Call your local emergency management office, animal shelter, or animal control office to get advice and information.

- If you are unable to return to your home right away, you may need to board your pet. Find out where pet boarding facilities are located. Be sure to research some outside your local area in case local facilities close.
- Most boarding kennels, veterinarians and animal shelters will need your pet's medical records to make sure all vaccinations are current. Include copies in your "pet survival" kit along with a photo of your pet.

Gary

- Note: Some animal shelters will provide temporary foster care for owned pets in times of disaster, but this should be considered only as a last resort.
- If you have no alternative but to leave your pet at home, there are some precautions you must take. Remember that leaving your pet at home alone can place your animal in great danger! Confine your pet to a safe area inside—NEVER leave your pet chained outside!
- Leave them loose inside your home with food and plenty of water. Remove the toilet tank lid, raise the seat and brace the bathroom door open so they can drink. Place a notice outside in a visible area, advising what pets are in the house and where they are located. Provide a phone number where you or a contact can be reached, as well as the name and number of your vet.

During a Disaster

- Bring your pets inside immediately.
- Have newspapers on hand for sanitary purposes. Feed the animals moist or canned food so they will need less water to drink.
- Animals have instincts about severe weather changes and will often isolate themselves if they are afraid. Bringing them inside early can stop them from running away. Never leave a pet outside or tied up during a storm.

- Separate dogs and cats. Even if your dogs and cats normally get along, the anxiety of an emergency situation can cause pets to act irrationally. Keep small pets away from cats and dogs.
- In an emergency, you may have to take your birds with you. Talk with your veterinarian or local pet store about special food dispensers that regulate the amount of food a bird is given. Make sure that the bird is caged and the cage is covered by a thin cloth or sheet to provide security and filtered light.

After a Disaster

- If after a disaster you have to leave town, take your pets with you. Pets are unlikely to survive on their own.
- In the first few days after the disaster, leash your pets when they go outside. Always maintain close contact. Familiar scents and landmarks may be altered and your pet may become confused and lost. Also, snakes and other dangerous animals may be brought into the area. Downed power lines are also a hazard.
- The behavior of your pets may change after an emergency. Normally quiet and friendly pets may become aggressive or defensive. Watch animals closely. Leash dogs and place them in a fenced yard with access to shelter and water.

(FROM THE FEDERAL EMERGENCY MANAGEMENT AGENCY (FEMA): HTTP://WWW.FEMA.GOV/PLAN/PREPARE/ANIMALS. SHTM)

You can find additional information on the Humane Society of the United States (HSUS) website. The HSUS Disaster Center has several useful disaster preparedness brochures available for download to help you plan for the needs of your pets, horses, and other animals during an emergency: http://www.hsus.org/web-files/PDF/DIST_DisasterPetBrochure.pdf.

Many other organizations, from the National Weather Service to PETA, also provide information regarding helping animals in an emergency on their websites.

Inseparable from the aftermath of a natural disaster is the mental and emotional toll such incidents create, especially as they extend into days, weeks, and longer. The final chapter in this book offers suggestions on how to deal with stress, how to keep you and your family amused, and how to cook and dine your way to the day when the lights finally come back on.

14

Handling the Stress

Beyond keeping yourself fed, there's another important challenge you'll face during an extended, multi-day sojourn without electrical power, and that is the psychological stress of the boredom, discomfort, frustration, and anxiety you're likely to experience. Officials are overworked. Tempers can flare, and not just waiting in line for water, but around the house among people who are ordinarily nice to each other. This is a chapter about how to tote all that emotional baggage. It will help you to prepare in advance for those times when you simply have to make the best of it.

Your World Upside Down

It's well known that long-term stress can produce a number of medical and emotional problems. Stress plays a role in 50 to 80 percent of our illnesses today, and over 40 million of us take drugs to cope with it. Stressed-out people are anxious, exhausted, irritable, and feel awful most of the time. Stress also weakens the immune system, raises blood pressure, increases your susceptibility to illness, and can even impair your judgment in emergency situations. However, after a disaster, natural or unnatural, you need to be thinking clearly.

You may as well accept it up front that getting the power back on may take time, and you're going to have to do without conveniences for a while. If you planned ahead, put together a pantry, gathered your Disaster Emergency Kit, acquired an alternative method for cooking, and have your home secured, you're halfway there.

Children Under Foot

Whatever you're going through, you can bet that the children are worse off than you are. They haven't yet matured enough to work themselves into a frenzy over a VISA bill. But there's more—unless you included (healthy) junk food in your Pantry Stash, they have suddenly been cut off from their daily comforts, too. They have no X-BOX or Playstation games to play, no DVDs or cable TV to watch, no computers, or Internet. They may not even be able to use their Magnificent Phone Devices. The streets are covered with broken branches and junk. Live power lines may be dangling everywhere, so you can't send them out to ride their skateboards or bikes. You also can't allow them to wander around on foot, lest they injure themselves.

To keep children (and yourselves) amused, it's a good idea to keep lots of games on hand. If they're old enough, you can even press the kids into helping with the cooking. Give them jobs. Show your little darlings how to sauté shallots or make pancakes. Let them know they're important to the family's survival. Who knows, they might take it seriously.

How to Relieve Stress

Sitting around with the power off is a perfect time to try some of these classic methods for relieving stress:

Exercise and Stretching: Do calisthenics in your yard. If the streets are safe, walk around and compare damage reports. It will almost always be true that a lot of people are worse off than you are. This can help you feel lucky and even inspire you to help the others in the neighborhood.

Yoga: Self-discipline can't be stressed enough in times like these. There's no time like the present to practice this ancient form of exercise and mental discipline.

Deep Breathing: Tension causes rapid, shallow breaths. So, to relax, change the pattern of your breathing. Inhale slowly, deliberately, and deeply; hold your breath; then exhale slowly. Count to eight during each round, and the temptation to strangle an indifferent official will pass.

Meditate: Finding the peace within you takes practice. Enjoy your memories of a time so long ago when your toast still popped out of your toaster; you had nothing better to do but grumble about e-mail spam; and you could watch your favorite *Survivor!* reruns on TV. Concentrate on the sights, smells, and sounds of the way life used to be. Or, indulge your senses in something entirely new: the blessed absence of all the above.

Massage: Depending on the nature of your relationships, take turns exchanging massages. Work the back of the neck and shoulders. Use thumbs and the heels of your hands.

Take Naps: Even a 15-minute nap can refresh you. For fun, try your nap in unusual places: the floor, the backyard, or on the dining room table.

Cook Your Stress Away

Cooking is another creative way to channel your frustration. Instead of sulking, whip up a batch of Asian-Style Vegetable Pancakes with Dipping Sauce (page 91) or Fire-Roasted Blueberry Cobbler (page 151). It'll keep everyone busy and creative, and reward you all with something delicious.

You can't solve major existential problems through cooking, but you can glow with pride as you solve minor ones: sautéing garlic in a cast iron skillet over a wood fire, frying a righteous breakfast over the whisper of a blue flame, or serving a hot three-course dinner using only one burner and one pan. All this helps pass the time, mainly by keeping everyone working together. The more courses, the less time you have to gripe.

But since you can't cook all the time, I'll share a secret: in addition to your Pantry Stash, you'll be glad to have these other diversions to occupy you between meals.

Play Games

To cope with life in general, you really ought to keep a variety of games handy, including board games, yard games, hide 'n' seek, and Scavenger Hunt, the Real Version.

With a deck of cards, you can play pinochle, poker, canasta, gin rummy, or solitaire. Consider playing Blackjack to see who will rake the yard, who will saw up branches, or who will drag the neighbor's lawnmower out of your swimming pool. Keep Monopoly and Scrabble at the ready, along with other games of skill and chance. Games that take time to play fill in the hours. Crafts such as knitting, crocheting, and beadwork can also help pass the time.

Read, Read, Read

When the last hurricane hit, I'd been so busy rewriting a novel, I realized that it had been months since I'd read one. On a trip to Manteo, North Carolina that summer, I had picked up Toni Morrison's *Sula,* her second book from 1973 that I'd been meaning to read since 1973. Thank you Professor Morrison for my day-long eavesdrop on Sula's world!

Robin and I caught up on a lot of reading after those storms. I reread back issues of *Publishers Weekly,* wept over *Romeo and Juliet,* and even dug out a dog-eared copy of *Hitchiker's Guide to the Galaxy*.

Napkin Folding

Artfully folded napkins are a dead giveaway that you are a cultured person with nothing to do. But even if you aren't, there's no denying that a well-set table without folded napkins is like a chain saw without two-stroke oil.

When there's no electricity, and your life seems light-years from "refined," perhaps that's the best time to consult the directions below and fold yourself some festive napkins. It's just one more way to thumb your nose at fate. You may be eating pantry cuisine, but darn it, your table is set with the best napkins this side of the Seine. It's also fun and educational for the kids—something you can learn together as a family. Best of all, after the lights come back on, it's a treasured skill that you will use for years to come.

"Yes," you can say proudly, as guests drool over your perfectly executed tri-folds, "I taught myself that particular napkin fold during Hurricane Yvonne back in '06."

For your first foray into the art of napkin folding, I've chosen a moderately challenging fold called the Pyramid. A starched cloth napkin is best, of course. But if all you have are paper napkins, you can certainly practice with those. Naturally, the sturdier the napkin, the better your folds will turn out.

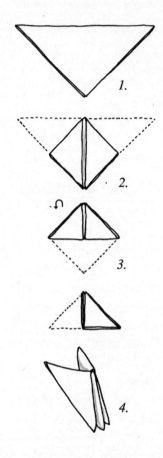

How to Fold the Pyramid

WHERE TO PLACE THE CUTLERY

Readers who were quick to judge the author as negligent for omitting instructions for proper table service in the main text of this guide will wax penitent upon seeing them here. According to the International Guild of Professional Butlers, you wouldn't want to be caught neglecting even one of these rules when setting cutlery on a table:

- The handles will be one inch from the edge of the table.
- The two outer-most pieces are used first.
- A soup spoon may go between knives if there is an appetizer before the soup.
- The butter knife on the bread plate has the blade face into the center of the plate.
- Only the soup course has one piece of flatware; all others have two. A salad should be torn into bite size pieces but a knife may be used to push the food onto the fork.

Overdoing Your Table

Now that you've mastered an impressive napkin fold, you're probably itching to set a table beautiful enough to feature your hard work. So, let's get right to it.

Study the diagram for a formal table setting below. You can trust this diagram, because it was provided by the International Guild of Professional Butlers*. It can be an amusing distraction to carefully observe the placement of dishes, glasses, and utensils. And it can make eating a simple meal a special event.

A. Napkin
B. Service plate
C. Soup bowl
D. Bread-and-butter plate with butter knife
E. Water glass
F. Wine glass
G. Wine glass
H. Salad fork
I. Dinner fork
J. Dessert fork
K. Knife
L. Teaspoon
M. Soup spoon

(*HTTP://WWW.BUTLERSGUILD.COM/INDEX.PHP?SUBJECT=89)

Whether you are just plain obsessive/compulsive or would like to steer your life in a new direction, follow these guidelines as you set up your backyard picnic table or sheet of plywood. The Butler's Guild is perfectly clear regarding the way in which the places are set: "Every place setting should be exactly the same, to the millimeter. An inexperienced butler might use some measuring device."

In the meantime, don't worry needlessly over the fact that your paper plates, napkins, and service are left over from your child's third birthday party. You are in an emergency situation and desperately trying to save your sanity here. Have fun.

During Hurricane Isabel, we compromised by using disposable dinnerware for breakfast and snacks. We did, however, reserve the "good dishes" for lunch and dinner. In our case, we were blessed with running water, so, to keep from going nuts, we were able to incorporate hand-washing dishes as part of our "busy-work" each day. Actually, after a day, we had to wash dishes with the garden hose out in the yard because the electric garbage disposal clogged from washing dishes in the sink. So we set up a trio of dishpans in the backyard, one with the dirty dishes, one for rinsing, and one for draining.

It's a Beautiful Day in the Neighborhood

Despite the misery, or perhaps because of it, disasters can bring out unexpected cooperation and charity between neighbors. Back in 1989, as Hugo's winds blasted the houses on Sullivan's Island, South Carolina, the Baker family (a made-up name) was huddled in the corner of their living room, fearful that they had made the wrong decision by staying home. Dad, Mom, and the two children were riding out the storm by the stone fireplace when they heard a scratching at the front door. Dad opened the door and in walked a family of squirrels. A dad, a mom, and two baby squirrels had applied for asylum and a door had opened unto them.

The furry family stepped cautiously along the wall and huddled in the corner across the room from the humans. While the tempest raged outside, neither species bothered the other, but shared the shelter and some mutual respect until the worst was over. When the door was once again opened, the refugees scampered up their tree, and life returned to normal.

In the aftermath of Isabel, we got to know our neighbors for the first time in eleven years. My wife and I tend to scurry into and out of our house like muskrats, anxious to get back to our work. After Isabel, everything changed. Half our neighborhood had ignored the warning to evacuate, and, like survivors emerging from the ruins in a B-movie, we picked our way into our front yards blinking around in slow motion at the wreckage, smiling the grateful smile of gamblers who have beaten the odds.

We'd had no idea that across the street lived a retired engineer. Next door was a pilot for the Navy Seals. Next to him was a medical doctor, and beyond were a police officer and a retired high-steel worker.

"And what do you do, Mr. and Mrs. Robertson?"

"We write words down. Sort of on paper."

"I mean for your job. Your work. What do you do for a living?"

"Well, sometimes people pay us."

Four doors down, I actually discovered a distant relative—the guy's great-great grandparents were also my great-great grandparents who had lived in northwestern Maine around 1888. Small world.

Silver Lining

In the face of adversity, people's hearts open wide. One guy brought his chain saw around to cut up problem limbs and branches. Another finagled a generator big enough for four families to run their refrigerators and watch a little TV. Everybody contributed their lawn mower gas to fuel the generator, and it worked great until the do-it-yourself tank farm ran dry. Gas stations can't pump gas without electricity. So much for the generator.

Another story comes from Hurricane Hugo about a reclusive chef forced by circumstances to feed the multitude. He was not a man of words, and still suffered emotional trauma from military service. Soft-spoken and shy, except when barking orders behind the cooking line, he found everyone in his devastated neighborhood unable to cope or organize themselves. They were all looking to him.

Painfully, he came out of his shell and took over. He ordered everyone to bring out their charcoal grills and line them up. He had them empty their refrigerators, bring out their salad fixings, condiments, bowls, plates, wines, and service. He created a cooking line and staffed it with passersby: a sommelier, a garde mange, a sous chef, grill cooks, waiters, and waitresses. Tables were set up inline for an impromptu banquet entitled "Eat it up before we throw it out." People came for blocks and ate royally while the food lasted, and for the chef, something inside him that had been broken for many years began to heal.

Go wander the streets like a Samaritan and see where you can help. See who needs what. Let others know what you need. Let the Disruptive Event turn your neighborhood into a real community. Make friends as you share resources and lend a hand. You can also organize group games or hold your own church service, prayer meeting, powwow, coffee klatch, sewing circle, sweat lodge, or encounter group. It would also be the perfect opportunity to introduce your neighbors to vegan food. Just pool your groceries, prepare a feast, break out the wine, and throw the best block party you will ever see again.

The Clouds Part

After more than a week without electricity, we sat reading and sweating beneath the patio umbrella. We were about to make lunch when we noticed a change in the air. It wasn't a new "something," it was the absence of a something. The noise had cranked down by 60db. Someone had turned off a generator. Then another. Then there was silence. Our next door neighbor poked his grinning face above the fence.

"The power's back on."

"Really?"

"No kidding. We're watching SpongeBob!"

Like Gollum lusting after the Ring, we raced back inside and turned on every light in the house. Flipped on the computer to check e-mail; turned on the TV; listened to the stereo; and browsed the Web. We reveled in the return of our precious work and play. Our beloved gadgets. Back again was our electric stove, toaster, and food processor. Back again were the reality shows, the commercials, the spyware, the pop-ups, and talking heads, top 40, golden oldies, and movies on DVD. We hurried to catch up on business e-mail and get back to our manuscripts and correspondence. Back to the rat race and responsibility, and the nine-to-five pressure of daily life. It all came back when the power lines hummed once again, and only then did we realize how much we had grown while the electricity was off.

Hurricane Isabel had given us another benefit, because it led to this book—a humble volume written by people who figured out a way to maximize comfort and eat impossibly good vegan meals after circumstances had rendered us powerless. We herewith pass this wisdom on to you.

Resources

Food and Cooking Supplies

Non-Perishable Foods

These sources offer a large variety of canned vegan meat alternatives, boxed mixes for vegan burgers, ribs, and seitan, and many other products.

Bob's Red Mill Whole Grain Store
www.bobsredmill.com
Phone: 800-349-2173

Cosmo's Vegan Shoppe
www.cosmosveganshoppe.com
Phone: 800-260-9968

Food Fight Grocery
www.foodfightgrocery.com
Phone: 503-233-3910

Mail Order Catalog for Healthy Eating
www.healthy-eating.com
Phone: 800-695-2241

Pangea
www.veganstore.com
Phone: 800-340-1200

Vegan Essentials
www.veganessentials.com
Phone: 866-88-VEGAN

Dehydrated or Freeze-Dried Foods

Harmony House Foods
www.harmonyhousefoods.com
A reliable source for dehydrated vegetables, fruits, and beans, they also carry freeze-dried fruits and vegetables, vegan soup blends, TVP, and nutritional yeast.
Phone: 800-696-1395

Harmony Valley Foods
http://harmonyvalleyfoods.com
Dehydrated vegan burger and sausage mixes—just add water.
Phone: 800-898-5457

DIY Food Dehydration

Making your own shelf-stable vegan meals is an great way to put up foods for an emergency if you have the time and a food dehydrator. If you want to explore this option, here are some sources for more information.

Food dehydrators: Prices on dehydrators begin at around $40, but don't expect them to perform as well as a premium unit, such as the Excalibur brand. Check out a variety of brands at Harvest Essentials (www.harvestessentials.com).

Books on dehydrating: As of the publication of this book, we could not find a strictly vegan dehydration manual; however, you can apply the principles from these books to plant-based products. For general instructions see *The Complete Dehydration Cookbook* by Mary Bell (Morrow, 1994).

For methods of creating your own vegan meals and snacks, see *Lipsmackin' Vegetarian Backpackin'* by Christine Conners and Tim Conners (Three Forks, 2004). In addition, many raw or living food cookbooks have sections on dehydrating food.

Portable Stoves

The stoves and gas canisters described in Chapter 4 can be found online or at your local restaurant supply or sporting goods store. To see a variety at a glance, Google "single burner butane stove" or go to Amazon.com and search "butane stove." See also www.frybake.com and www.coleman.com.

Emergency Supplies

The following companies provide emergency kits for home, office, and car, including pre-packed foods, first-aid, and safety equipment. The individual descriptions highlight additional specific features offered by each company.

The American Red Cross
(See Official Agencies below)

Disaster Necessities
www.disasternecessities.com

Emergency equipment and food storage. 72-hour kits, water storage supplies, first-aid kits, and educational materials. See the catalog and contact information is available on the website.
Phone: 435-602-6853
E-mail: help@DisasterNecessities.com

Emergency Preparedness Center
www.areyouprepared.com
Emergency survival kits for home, car, school, office. Kits for individuals and two to four persons. See catalog and

contact information on the website.
Phone: 1-888-654-3447
E-mail: Sales@the7store.net

Homeland Preparedness
www.homelandpreparedness.com
Emergency supplies, disaster kits, and survival gear. You're not likely to find vegan foods here, but they sell great hand-crank lights and battery chargers as well as emergency preparedness kits for dogs and cats (also see QuakeKare.com below).
Phone: 800-350-1489
E-mail: service@homelandpreparedness.com

Pack Lite Foods
www.packlitefoods.com
A source for vegetarian freeze-dried back packing meals, with some vegan choices including: curry lentil soup, minestrone, and chili.
Phone: 541-410-3481
E-mail: mondt@boreal.org

QuakeKare
www.quakekare.com
Provides emergency preparedness kits for all types of disasters that include fanny packs, foods, solar and hand-crank lights and radios. Kits are available for earthquakes, hurricanes, fires, floods, and other disasters. Also has emergency kits for cats and dogs.
Phone: 800-277-3727
E-mail: info@QuakeKare.com

SafetyMax
www.safetymax.com
Offers a full line of first aid, survival, and safety products and training services. Office survival equipment and kits for first responders, backpackers, and survival kits for 2 to 10 people.
Phone: 800-585-8506
E-mail: info@safetymax.com

The Ready Store
www.thereadystore.com
Survival kits, water storage, communications products, and other emergency preparedness items. Their freeze-dried and ready-to-eat meals aren't vegan, but they do carry some vegan ingredients such as freeze-dried vegetables and fruits.
Phone: 800-773-5331
E-mail: customerservice@thereadystore.com

Major Surplus and Survival
www.majorsurplus.com
You won't likely find anything vegan here, food-wise, but the range of emergency and survival supplies is astounding.
Phone: 800-441-8855 or 310-324-8855
E-mail: CustomerCare@MajorSurplus.com

Official Agencies

For information about hurricanes:
NOAA/ National Weather Service
National Centers for Environmental Prediction
National Hurricane Center / Tropical Prediction Center
www.nhc.noaa.gov

For information about weather emergencies:
NOAA/ National Weather Service
National Centers for Environmental Prediction
Storm Prediction Center
www.spc.noaa.gov

For tornado information by state:
www.disastercenter.com/tornado.html

For information about earthquake activity:
U.S. Department of the Interior
U.S. Earthquake Center
http://earthquake.usgs.gov/

For information on investigations into power blackouts:
The Federal Energy Regulatory Commission
E-mail: customer@ferc.gov
Telephone: 202-502-6088
Toll-free: 1-866-208-3372
http://www.ferc.gov (search: "blackout")

For first-aid kits and other products:
American Red Cross National Headquarters
2025 E Street, NW
Washington, DC 20006
Phone: (202) 303 5000
www.redcross.org
Find local chapters by clicking "Find Local Chapter" at: http://www.redcross.org/contactus (enter your zip code at the prompt)

FEMA
Federal Emergency Management Agency
Phone: 1 (800) 621-FEMA (3362)
www.fema.gov/

Important Phone Numbers

Record important phone numbers here, to have them handy in the case of an emergency.

Ambulance _____

Fire _____

Police _____

Family Physician: _____ Phone: _____

Local Hospital: _____ Phone: _____

Power Company: _____

Gas Company: _____

Water Company: _____

Home Insurance: _____

Auto Insurance: _____

Federal Emergency Management Agency: (800) 621-FEMA (3362)

American Red Cross: (local chapter) _____

Veterinarian: _____

Animal Shelter: _____

Other: _____

Index

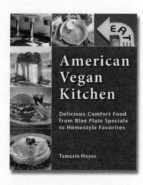

American Vegan Kitchen
Delicious Comfort Food from Blue Plate Specials to Homestyle Favorites

by Tamasin Noyes

Do you ever crave the delicious comfort foods served at your local diner, deli, or neighborhood cafe? This cookbook shows you how to make vegan versions of your favorite dishes in your own home kitchen.

These 200+ recipes will satisfy vegans and non-vegans alike with deli sandwiches, burgers and fries, mac and cheese, pasta, pizza, omelets, pancakes, soups and salads, casseroles, and desserts. Enjoy truly great American flavors from tempting ethnic dishes to the homestyle comfort foods of the heartland.

The book contains eight pages of full-color photos and helpful icons to bring American comfort food home to your table.

For more about Tamasin Noyes, visit her blog at:
www.veganappetite.com.

Vegan Heritage Press
Paperback, 268 pages,
7½ x 9
ISBN: 978-0-9800131-0-8

Vegan Fire & Spice
200 Sultry and Savory Global Recipes

by Robin Robertson

Take a trip around the world with delicious, mouth-watering vegan recipes ranging from mildly spiced to nearly incendiary. Explore the spicy cuisines of the U.S., South America, Mexico, the Caribbean, Europe, Africa, the Middle East, India, and Asia with *Red-Hot White Bean Chili, Jambalaya, Szechuan Noodle Salad, Vindaloo Vegetables*, and more.

Organized by global region, this book gives you 200 inventive and delicious, 100% vegan recipes for easy-to-make international dishes, using readily available ingredients. Best of all, you can adjust the heat yourself and enjoy these recipes hot – or not.

For more about Robin Robertson's cookbooks, visit her website www.globalvegankitchen.com or blog at: http://veganplanet.blogspot.com.